Praise for *Your Secret Calling*

Your Secret Calling .... the whole Gospel. Leanna .... fully grasp how good God is .... can be. We have too little God-directed ou............... be the light to the world and empower others. You ... discover how to hear the call of God and act on it. God wants to release your full potential as you unlock the key truths revealed in this book.

— ***Jeffrey H. Coors***
Chairman, Intercessors for America
Retired Chairman, Graphic Packaging International

In the many years I have known her, Leanna Cinquanta has proven to be an incredibly courageous mover and shaker. Her new book carries her heart—the heart of a true reformer. *Your Secret Calling* is an invaluable guide for individuals and leaders alike. You will be empowered to make a lasting impact and transformative change in an increasingly dark and despairing world. By implementing these "keys" on a large scale, the body of Christ is being called to ignite the most significant move of God in history!

— ***Dr. Ché Ahn***
Senior Leader, Harvest Rock Church, Pasadena, CA
President, Harvest International Ministry
International Chancellor, Wagner University

Your Secret Calling will stir everything in you and call you to action. Leanna's teaching and real-life stories are riveting, impartational, and faith-empowering. A must-read.

— ***Patricia King***
Author, Minister, Media Producer, and Host
www.patriciaking.com

We live in an extraordinary time in history, where followers of Jesus must come up higher and confront accelerating evil, perversion and corruption. Few authors better describe our "wounded world" with the riveting, true stories Leanna shares. Then she gives undeniable validation that those stories can be changed to hope and glorious transformation. Cutting-edge biblical truths disclose the long-hidden fullness of our identity and empower us into God's best. *Your Secret Calling* is a clarion call to step into a realm where the miraculous and the mundane intersect, sparking a divine momentum of spiritual and tangible thriving for which our wounded world yearns.

— ***Dr. Ralph Plumb*** *Kingdom Alliances Sourcing*
Financial, Human & Intellectual Capital
https://drralphplumb.com

Having known Dr. Leanna for over two decades, I can attest that her passion for Christ has led her to a clear understanding and practice of a hermeneutic known as historical/eschatological dualism. Simply stated, it is biblical understanding of the kingdom of God whereby the kingdom is both here today in its practical application and at the same time the Kingdom is coming with the soon return of the King, Who will make right all of creation. Leanna deftly challenges believers, "Dare to find Your Secret Calling." Examples within these pages will demonstrate to children of the Kingdom how meeting people at their point of earthly need while sharing the news of our great Lord, will accelerate our eternal impact.

*— **Dr. Thomas E. Hatley***
Senior Pastor, Emmanuel Baptist Church, Rogers, AR
Former Chairman, SBC International Mission Board

In every heart is a longing, "How can I make a difference? What is my highest purpose?" *Your Secret Calling* is a God-sent answer to that heart cry. In 2011 Dr. Leanna Cinquanta was one of the most promising and prolific graduates of our doctoral program at Regent University. Her international success in ministry fields considered impenetrable testifies to the power that is released when we discover and live the whole, undiminished Gospel. Are you ready to be equipped for a life with eternal consequence? This inspiring Christ-centered book holds your key to purpose, abundance, fruitfulness, and impact.

*— **Dr. James T. Flynn***
Associate Dean, Regent University School of Divinity

At a moment in history where Christians are generally afraid to face the difficult questions, Leanna Cinquanta courageously gives answers. With great clarity about the ideological roots of evil and suffering, Leanna tells story after story of the power of the Gospel of the kingdom of God to transform lives and communities.

Your Secret Calling is filled with wisdom and illustrations of how we move from enslavement to freedom, from poverty to human flourishing, from the darkness of the Devil's empire to the glorious light of the kingdom of God.

Having worked for over four decades with organizations that address poverty and under development, I can testify that Leanna has written the most clearly articulated account that I have ever read about the potential of everyday people to transform brokenness to wholeness and lack to plenty, and in the process, find their own highest purpose.

At a time when the church needs to awaken from her slumber, *Your Secret Calling* provides a wakeup call through bold vision and initiatives. This book gives a model for individuals and the church to follow our Lord as He dispels evil, illumines darkness and yes, empowers His Church to prevail against the very gates of Hell. This book is enthusiastically recommended!

— ***Darrow Miller***
Author of Disciplining Nations: The Power of Truth
to Transform Culture
Co-Founder Disciple Nations Alliance

YOUR *Secret* CALLING

YOUR
Secret
CALLING

Ancient Keys to Unleash
God's Highest Purpose

LEANNA CINQUANTA

ILLUMIFY
MEDIA.COM

YOUR Secret CALLING

Copyright © 2024 by Leanna Cinquanta

All rights reserved. No part of this book may be reproduced in any form or by any means—whether electronic, digital, mechanical, or otherwise—without permission in writing from the publisher, except by a reviewer, who may quote brief passages in a review.

Unless otherwise noted, all Scripture is from the Holy Bible, New International Version®, NIV® Copyright ©1973, 1978, 1984, 2011 by Biblica, Inc.® Used by permission. All rights reserved worldwide.

Scripture marked ASV is taken from the American Standard Version.

Scripture marked NASB is from the New American Standard Bible®, Copyright © 1960, 1971, 1977, 1995 by The Lockman Foundation. All rights reserved.

Scripture marked NKJV is taken from the New King James Version®. Copyright © 1982 by Thomas Nelson. Used by permission. All rights reserved.

Throughout this book, some names have been changed for the sake of privacy.

The views and opinions expressed in this book are those of the author and do not necessarily reflect the official policy or position of Illumify Media Global.

Published by
Illumify Media Global
www.IllumifyMedia.com
"Let's bring your book to life!"

Paperback ISBN: 978-1-959099-88-8

Typeset by Art Innovations (http://artinnovations.in/)
Cover design by Debbie Lewis

Printed in the United States of America

CONTENTS

Foreword   xi
Introduction   xv

PART I   Receive The Ancient Keys

1. The Secret Goodness   3
2. Your Triune Royalty   13
3. A Wounded World   24
4. Unshrinking Jesus   39
5. De-Fragmenting the Gospel   49
6. Case Study – Suicide to Shalom   60
7. The Mystery Church   72
8. Case Study – Welfare to Well-Being   92

PART II   Unleash God's Highest Purpose

9. Your Secret Power   103
10. Case Study – Evil Versus the Ekklesia   126
11. Mind Shifts And the Three-P Key   140
12. Case Study: Segregated to Influential   154
13. Unleashing the Ekklesia   161
14. The Key to Exponential Good   182
15. Enter Your Secret Calling   198

Endnotes   210
Bibliography   217
About the Author   218

FOREWORD

Can the Church Disciple Nations?

Attempt great things for God, expect great things from God was the motto of British cobbler William Carey. Two centuries after him, it has become easier to appreciate the fact that his faith and service made Carey the father of modern India.

The "secrets" that Leanna Cinquanta unwraps in her powerful book were known to Christians that reformed corrupt Europe and transformed its colonies into modern USA and Canada. They discipled nations because they knew that the Light of the world would overcome darkness.

Babylonian Emperor Nebuchadnezzar had defeated, killed, and enslaved the parents of Daniel, Ezekiel, Zerubabbel, Haggai, Ezra, Zechariah, and Nehemiah. These men grew up among exiles who had lost all hope for their nation. After Solomon's temple was destroyed, Israelites saw their nation as nothing but a valley of dry bones (Ezekiel 37:1-10). That is why God asked, "Can these bones live?"

Against external odds and an internal mood of defeat, humble men of faith took great risks. They returned to a devastated city to rebuild God's temple and kingdom. They knew the secret, "The people that do know their God shall be strong, and do exploits." (Daniel 11:32 KJV).

Knowing that the living God is sovereign, that He is seated above all powers and principalities, enabled believers to go into the fiery furnace and the lions' den. Believers took action. They didn't seek escape.

One argument against William Carey's call for missions was that the heathen will kill you because they are without the fear of God and the rule of law. In response, Carey asked a counter question in his seminal book *Enquiry*: Is the awful state of the lawless heathen an argument *against* missions or *for* missions? If not the knowledge of God, then what else could possibly reform hearts and heal nations?

Carey's readers knew what our generation has forgotten. The Irish were barbaric. They abducted and enslaved St. Patrick when he was a young boy. Guided by a dream, their slave escaped only to return to the slave owners as St Patrick. Thomas Cahill's book *How The Irish Saved Civilization* (1995) describes how the knowledge of God transformed the Irish. They went out to evangelize and educate a disintegrating Western Europe.

Why did Apostle Paul accept frequent persecutions and imprisonments in order to turn the kingdom of darkness upside down? He knew the second "secret" unwrapped in this book. Our generation needs to relearn the whole, unmitigated Gospel that inspired emancipators like John Wesley, William Wilberforce, Amy Carmichael, Catherine Booth, and Dr. Martin Luther King Jr. to lay down their lives plowting tough soils and planting the seeds of God's kingdom.

Our generation, confused about its own identity, can be metamorphosed by the knowledge that the Lamb of God shed his blood to purchase Satan's slaves to make them God's sons. Sonship is kingship—if your father happens to be the King. He saves sinners to lift them up, to sit with him in the heavenly realm, commissioning them for a royal purpose.

Can the Church disciple nations? The answer is *yes* when we discover our secret destiny that allies redemptive priestly service with reformational kingly stewardship.

The book in your hands is not another academic treatise with interesting insights. The "secrets" that Leanna Cinquanta unfolds have already turned dead, dry bones into thriving havens of abundant life. This book is packed with dynamite that can blow up the West's escapist theology and resurrect your long-dormant calling.

April 18, 2024

—*Vishal Mangalwadi*
Author of *This Book Changed Everything:
The Bible's Amazing Impact on Our World*
www.RevelationMovement.com
www.TruthMatters.tv
Facebook: Vishal Mangalwadi

INTRODUCTION

"All of you!" bellowed Najjad. "Move it! Get in that room before I count to five or I'll slit his throat." Najjad slammed the trafficker's head against the wall and pressed a knife blade to his jugular. The criminal uttered a terrified gurgle as the others hurried to obey. Then, pushing the trafficker into the room too, Najjad bolted the door, locking them all inside.

Drawing several deep breaths, Najjad sheathed his weapon. The fury in his eyes began to subside replaced by a no-less-intense urgency. "Let's find the kids. No time to lose." A quick scouting of dingy corridors revealed small, dark bedrooms. Stuffed inside each were about eight miserable children, both boys and girls. Some were as young as six or eight years old. The children were malnourished and had rashes on their skin from lack of proper hygiene.

The trafficker had a history of abducting and selling children. The girls would become sex slaves, raped by up to eleven men a day. To fuel a lewd market for cheap organ transplants, the boys' kidneys, livers, and hearts would be ripped from their bodies. The trafficker and his team had brainwashed the older children by promising to provide what their impoverished rural parents could not, a good education.

They were all so traumatized that they didn't know who to trust, so they refused to go with Najjad to freedom! He hadn't expected that.

Overpowering the trafficker turned out to be the easy part! How might these abused, terrified children be convinced to come with him to safety? Time was running out. The trafficker and his crew might escape from the room at any moment.

Najjad persuaded the thirty-three children to gather together in one of the rooms, and sitting cross-legged on the floor with them, he looked into their eyes. The love that drove him here, that propelled him to risk his life for them, rose up in his heart. Each of these little lives stood at a cruel crossroads they should never have had to face. They were on the brink of either destruction or hope. Himself a native of the children's home region, he began to speak to them in their own local dialect.

But the children remained stalwart. The older ones had suffered the worst brainwashing by the trafficker. "Don't tell anyone what is happening here," the trafficker had threatened. "And if you try to run away, I will kill you, and also your family."

"These people are criminals," Najjad explained. "They have been hurting you, and you are hungry. Is that right? "

Little heads nodded.

"They are planning to hurt you more. I'm here to rescue you. I am your brother. Please trust me."

The banging from inside the locked room reverberated down the corridor. In no time the trafficker and his cronies would escape and come attack Najjad and reclaim the children.

※ ⋅⋅ ※

Sometimes you don't even want to look at the headlines; "another child abducted and killed," "another suicide," "another overdose." Your heart cries out that something is wrong. If Jesus is the Prince of Peace, why is there so much turmoil? If Jesus is the Light of the World, why is the world so full of darkness? If God is good, why does he permit these atrocities? Christians ask, "Why aren't we making more of a difference?"

Sadly, many believers have been conditioned to think salvation is all there is to being a Christian. Work or hobbies are considered "secular" and prayer "spiritual." Beyond a bit of charity, we conclude it's not important to make a difference in this earthly realm, since what really matters is the spiritual. We look for opportunities to share our faith in the workplace, but does our actual work or profession itself have any value in God's economy? Are the two exclusive of each other and unrelated?

On the opposite end of the spectrum are those who try to right the world's wrongs but lay aside the message of salvation, or whose mouths confess Christ while their lifestyles deny him.

Many people today, especially young generations, consider Christian faith outdated and irrelevant. At best it is perceived as just another set of dos and don'ts, and at worst a bastion of hypocrisy or of opposition to a changing culture. Meanwhile depression, suicide, crime and addictions hold precious souls in bondage to destruction.

People wonder "what is my purpose? What is my calling? How can my life make a difference?" Pastors cogitate over their church's apparent lack of influence while entrepreneurs and other leaders wonder if their business has any eternal value. Some ask, "Is the missionary important to God, but not the mechanic, the mail carrier or a marketer? Does not the work of the pharmacist, property manager, and police officer have eternal value as does that of the pastor?"

Believers pray that many may come to know Christ and have eternal life in heaven. But our hearts long for something more - for some expression of heaven to come to earth as well. Yes, it will happen in full when Jesus returns. But what about now?

The disappointment, confusion, and disillusionment suffered by human beings, junior or senior, Christ followers or otherwise, share a common cause: we have been seeing and operating out of a diminished reality. "The gospel we proclaim has been shrunk."[1]

Deep down we know we were born for a great and beautiful reason. That longing is the Spirit of our Heavenly Father saying, "Yes! There is more! Let me take you there." That glimpse of glory caught by our yearning heart is nothing other than the secret of the ages. Tactfully concealed for centuries by the sinister agenda of spiritual wickedness, the secret is none other than this: God's highest purpose on Planet Earth and the part we play in it, our calling.

The reason for which we have not perceived it is simple: we have so rarely stepped back and looked at the big picture of the Bible. When we do so, ancient keys emerge which unlock the mystery!

Jesus came that "whoever believes in him shall not perish but have eternal life." This same Jesus also declared, "I have come that they may have life and have it in abundance!" He came "to heal the brokenhearted . . . to set at liberty those who are oppressed." He came "to destroy the devil's work."

But our shrunken understanding of God, ourselves, and life itself have diminished and divided these great passages into either spiritual or physical. Our programming has blocked us from seeing the glorious wholeness of the Bible. It has blinded us to our awesome God who made both spirit and flesh, both this world and the next… and this blindness locks us out of our secret calling!

The tragic fruit of this partial truth is a stunted experience of our destiny, and a world full of people who remain, like the trafficked children, in bondage to destruction.

In rare seasons great waves of revival, whole-society healing, and abundant life burst upon certain geographies and peoples. Brothels and strip clubs go bankrupt because those who once patronized them no longer desire the things of darkness. Husbands who used to drink away their earnings and abuse their families instead bring home food for their children and treat their wives with honor. Thousands turn to Christ, repenting of sin.

These occasional movements come to pass despite the fact that God's people, those through whom he intended to work, see only a dim vision of his end goal. Still operating in our diminished reality, our shrunken gospel, in many cases we inadvertently oppose God's bigger vision. Oblivious to his highest purpose, we are not in a state of mind or spirit for him to fulfill it through us. Therefore precious souls victimized by the works of darkness remain enslaved and we miss out on our highest calling.

Our secret calling has been concealed partly by the wisdom of God, who chooses to elucidate his mysteries each at its appointed time. Cracks and blemishes overlaid through centuries of attempted interpretation and good intentions have obscured it further. On rare occasions the secret has been sighted but sometimes misinterpreted, other times avoided.

What will happen when we apprehend the big picture of the Bible and begin to allow God to fulfill through us, with eyes wide open and heart full of anticipation, his highest purpose?

Your Secret Calling presents ancient keys to open a dam that has for centuries restrained a glorious deluge of God's goodness. This tidal wave of abundant life can ignite the redemption of billions of souls, the ending of poverty and oppression, and the healing of nations. You are invited to experience a biblically sound paradigm shift, to embark on a rarely-trodden pathway. You'll be unleashed into the joy and influence you knew you were made for but could never quite lay hold of.

Church leaders, when you apply the concepts in this book you will exit the vicious circle of irrelevancy. Not only will your church become an "essential service" that people are irresistibly drawn to and transformed by; your congregation will also radiate God's goodness with such brilliance as to drive back the powers of darkness that are wreaking havoc in your city.

Businesspersons, homemakers, and marketplace professionals, you'll be released from the sense that work and play is of little interest to God. Your skills, your talents, your hobbies are anointed! Thriving in your workplace, developing wealth, raising a family, and influencing this world for good are not just important; they are radically essential parts of God's plan.

Let me take a moment to assert that *Your Secret Calling* does not promote Christian Reconstructionism, which aims to impose Old Testament law on modern society, nor Dominionism, which purports that Christians are to influence through top-down control mechanisms. It does not endorse the "social gospel," which prioritizes social action at the expense of proclaiming salvation through faith in Jesus Christ.

If you're not yet a follower of Christ, I believe you're going to encounter God in a natural, non-religious way that answers your deepest questions. Perhaps for the first time you'll be able to say, "Now I can believe that God is, and that he is good. Now I see who I am and where I fit. Now I am ready to enter my adventure hand in hand with my Father."

If you're a follower of Christ, this book is written in such a way that every Christian tribe—Catholic and Calvinist, Presbyterian and Pentecostal, Anglican, Apostolic and Adventist, Baptist and Orthodox, Methodist and non-denominational and every other expression of Christ's body—can relate, engage and be launched into a greater experience of God's goodness.

To unleash you into this adventure, I am grateful to stand on the shoulders of others who have made profound contributions, revealing a more full understanding of God, ourselves and our purpose. *Your Secret Calling* allows the Holy Scriptures to unfurl a concealed pathway that is simple, yet earthshaking. Along the way inspiring testimonies and practical case studies illustrate how you can apply the truths that are being revealed, and be the catalyst of transformed lives, cities and nations.

※ ✦ ※

Najjad cast a desperate glance at his colleague and breathed a prayer. "Lord, help these children to trust us."

Just then a little girl stepped forward. Her hair dangled in ropes about her dirt-smeared face, and scabs had formed under the perpetual discharge oozing from each nostril. The color of her clothes, unwashed since her abduction, was almost obscured by caked-on filth. She approached Najjad and looked straight into his face. Then, with a swift and decisive motion, she threw her arms around him. He embraced her and held her as tears wetted both their cheeks. "Please take us home," she sobbed.

It was as if a key had been inserted into their hearts. Suddenly all the children ran to Najjad. Now they were ready to trust him. But there was no time to waste . . .

Najjad and his teammate had hired two large buses. Once outside with the children, they began the arduous three-day journey back home over treacherous mountain roads. All the children were safely reunited with their families. For many years thereafter, WIN (We Ignite Nations) sponsored their education so they could receive the schooling they dreamed of while remaining safe from traffickers.[2]

The twenty-seven-year-old hero in this story is WIN's national coordinator for that region. Today he and our other heroic native leaders continue to rescue trafficking victims and spearhead WIN's innovative sustainable solutions that put an end to poverty and bring Christ's love to remote and neglected regions.

※ ✦ ※

The trafficked children are like the people and the world around us, captives of a cruel tyrant, on a path to destruction. Spiritual lostness, war, slavery, addictions, suicide, depression, and poverty are some of the symptoms.

But these victims can be rescued!

The audacious rescue of the children started with one person who lived out his secret calling.

Like Najjad, you are powerful. You can experience a life of wholeness, confidence, fulfillment and joy. But that's not all! God has placed in you not just the seeds of personal triumph but also of public influence. You're reading this book because you have a magnificent destiny and you're not content to sit idle and let it pass you by. You believe you have a high calling! But it's secret, veiled, unfulfilled.

What will happen when you discover it? What will happen when God's highest purpose is unleashed through you? The following pages will take you into the adventure that has waited for centuries to be revealed. The secret keys to unleash this life-giving torrent are about to be placed in your hands.

PART I

RECEIVE THE ANCIENT KEYS

"The earth is the Lord's, and everything in it."
—Psalm 24:1

"Many modern-day Christians have lost touch with the all-encompassing gospel that goes beyond personal salvation and reaches every corner of society."
—David Kinnaman

1

THE SECRET GOODNESS

"God saw all that He had made, and it was very good."
—Gen. 1:31

"We have misunderstood the concept of the Lordship of Christ over the whole of man and the whole of the universe and have not taken to us the riches that the Bible gives us for ourselves, for our lives and for our culture."
—Francis Schaeffer

At seven years old I beheld my first agate. Captivated by its beauty, I became an avid collector of the rare mineral orbs. With eyes honed to grasp the faintest telltale translucent hue, I could spy an agate from some distance away. My parents feared I would become a hunchback from perpetually scanning the ground. With wonderment my fingertips explored the smooth surface where pristine white lines swirled and arced, sometimes encircling a center crowned with gleaming crystals.

Agates seemed to me like a piece of something royal, even divine—a gift from another realm, extraterrestrial, unexplainable, magnetic in a strange way that wooed my inmost being. But what lay between the white lines captivated my senses the most. The translucent red, grey, or black between the lines allowed me to see in . . . but only dimly. From that mysterious depth a sweetness beckoned, "There's more. Look deeper. Here is concealed a secret."

Mystery Between the Lines

At age fifteen I discovered the divine Gift. I met Jesus . . . literally . . . face-to-face. The heart-pounding account is detailed in my book *Treasures in Dark Places*. The sense of awe I had experienced when gazing at an agate foreshadowed the wonder of encountering the great Agate, the treasure beyond all treasures, Love incarnate, God himself. Believers are "in Christ" (2 Cor. 5:17). So now I was "in" the "Agate, redeemed by his grace, empowered by his Holy Spirit, and secure in knowing I was now an heir of eternal life.

But there was more.

Through the years, as I imbibed the Bible, discovered the character and heart of God, and grew in my relationship with Jesus, I perceived that the mystery of God contained a hidden dimension. This clandestine treasure was either little discussed or only alluded to in passing. More lay "between the lines" of Jesus the Agate, and I was missing it. The books I read were missing it. The sermons and Bible teachings I heard were missing it. The church was missing it. And therefore, the whole world was being deprived of a secret part of God and of humankind that would make our lives a hundred times more joyous, victorious, and purposeful.

Most of my life has been vested in discovering deeper dimensions of this secret, delving deeper "between the lines" of God's goodness and our place in his purpose. I have stood in awe as ancient keys emerged from the pages of the Scriptures.

As the founder and president of the organization WIN (We Ignite Nations),[1] I've had the opportunity to apply these discoveries to real-life situations in some of the most difficult and dark environments. WIN's amazing team of heroes has been using these ancient keys for twenty-five years, and we've witnessed what happens when God's highest purpose is unleashed.

WIN focuses on places where many still have no access to the knowledge of Christ, places which also rank among the world's worst in poverty, slavery, human trafficking, and racism. One of these regions was once called the "graveyard of Christianity" and a "poisonous hub of human trafficking." Yet as people just like you discover and live out their secret calling, even here human trafficking is being defeated, poverty driven back, and the infirm and addicted delivered into new and abundant life. Not through charity, but through sustainable initiatives that build both human dignity and economic strength.

People are being redeemed into eternal life and also abundant life now, reversing spiritual, physical, and emotional poverty.

You may be experiencing your life as the drab, dull exterior surface of what would appear to be a common piece of granite. You're getting along, living day by day, making the best of it . . . but you keep wondering, "Isn't there something greater below the surface? Is there no treasure on the other side of the mundane? Are there no greater heights to which I am summoned? And if so, how do I cross over? Where do I begin?"

A secret calling awaits you! Like a proud father eager for his child to unwrap a gift, God waits with joyous expectation for you, his special creation, to apprehend this mystery. When you do, his highest purpose for your life will be unleashed, catapulting you into the adventure for which you were created!

But right now, your secret calling lies concealed behind multiple layers of misconceptions and partial truths propagated not directly by humans or institutions, for we have all been the victim of an ancient cover-up. The enemy is "spiritual forces of evil in the heavenly realms," but the victory is already secure (Eph. 6:12)!

Apprehending this treasure begins with a paradigm shift. The ability to see the mystery between the lines of the agate and experience the full power of God's highest purpose, must start by exposing, one by one, new layers of his truth, new dimensions of your destiny.

Theologian and historian Vishal Mangalwadi declares, "The Bible created the modern world of science and learning because it gave us the Creator's vision of what reality is all about."[2] The Bible holds the pathway to life, revealing ancient keys to unlock your glorious inheritance. The first are contained in the first chapters of Genesis.

The Creator, Author of Life

The first words in the Bible's first chapter are "In the beginning God created" (Gen. 1:1). As the origin of all things, God is the author of life.[3] The Creator is the first and greatest scientist and artist. If uncoiled, the DNA in the human body would reach to the sun and back six hundred times! The human brain contains one hundred billion neurons that pass signals to each other via a thousand trillion synapses. Darwin promoted overt racism and the dehumanizing theory of "favoured races."[4] Nevertheless atheistic attempts to explain our origins sans God have become mainstream. To some it appears that science is "at war" with faith. However modern science itself came into being in the sixteenth century due to the resurgence of a Christian worldview. Non-Christian philosophers have called Christian faith the "mother of science"[5] while Galileo, a devout believer, is considered the "father of modern science."[6] God is the great and immutable scientist. Genuine science is the human endeavor to understand the limitless intricacy of the original Scientist's brilliant mind and creative genius.

Our Heavenly Father, the Source of Love

Our creator is not a distant power or impersonal force. He is our Father. This Father is not abusive or austere, neither violent nor absent. He is *good*. He is holy, perfect in every way, the essence and origin of love, justice, mercy, and grace. "I will be a Father to you, and you will be my sons and daughters, says the Lord Almighty" (2 Cor. 6:18). God desires the best for human beings and for all of his creation.

Some people ask, "If God is our good and loving Father, why does he let bad things happen to us?"

Suppose a father locked his son in a room for days on end to keep him from ever making a mistake. Is that love? Would we say he is a good father? No! Our heavenly Father grants us freedom to choose right or wrong. As we'll soon see, evil is a consequence of humans making wrong choices and thus misusing our freedom. What should amaze us is not that bad things happen, but that God is such a good and loving Father as to make a way for us to be delivered from the consequences of our wrong choices . . . as we'll soon see. He is not behind us with a stick and a scowl, saying, "Get yourself out of the mud." Instead, he is reaching out with a great big, proud Daddy smile calling, "Take my hand, precious child. I'll lead you into your best!"

> Be liberated from the misbelief that you are an orphan. You have a Father who adores you.

Creation Is Good

Seven times in the first chapter of the Bible, created things are summed up with the rich Hebrew word *tov* meaning good, beautiful, and bountiful.[7] As the Creator is good, so is his handiwork. But across the ages human society has strayed into two extremes: Eastern worldviews worship the creation as if it was the creator and see everything as containing an element of the divine. A variation of this gives us modern pluralism's "there's no absolute truth." Dualism is the opposite extreme. Inherited from the Greeks, this view, known as the sacred-secular divide, sees creation and physical activities as "secular" and therefore a potential distraction from that which "really" matters, the spiritual.

> Be liberated from lobotomizing life in the name of spirituality. All that our good God created is good.

But when we accept that God is totally good, then of course what he creates must also be good. God's spirit is the source of life and gives birth to the physical, and both realms in unison receive one undivided approval.

King of All, Wellspring of Liberty

Because God is Spirit, people sometimes wonder whether he is interested in our everyday circumstances. It is easier for us to believe he is active in the spirit realm—eternity and heaven—but harder to conceive of him as engaged in the now, the life that swirls around us every day. This is too small a view of God, because he is not only loving Father and Creator of life; He is also King—and as our King, he invites us into liberty—a responsible, engaged kind of freedom that celebrates and promotes what is right and good and just.

There is no limit on a king's jurisdiction. He reigns over everything!

Farmer John and his family worked from dawn to dusk to eke out a living from growing crops in their field. One day a truck drove up and two men got out. "We think there may be oil under your field," they said. Farmer John agreed to let them drill. When they struck oil, they said, "You own the land above the oil, where you cultivate your corn and potatoes. But we are the ones who drilled into the soil and found oil. So the oil is ours." Farmer John said, "No, the oil is mine!" The judge ruled in favor of the farmer who became an overnight millionaire . . . because he owned all of his land—both the surface and what was underneath.

> The spiritual births the physical, but seen and unseen both matter. Life belongs to God. He created it. You're part of it. Rejoice in all of it!

In a far greater way, a king doesn't just reign only in his palace or over the military or navy. God owns the fields, the cattle, the industry, and reigns over all the people (Psalm 24:1, 50:10). God cares about everything—what is seen and unseen, material and immaterial.

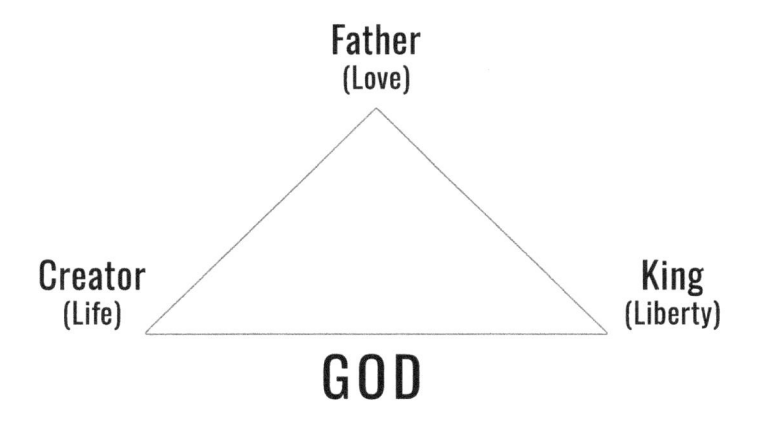

```
              Father
              (Love)
               /\
              /  \
             /    \
            /      \
   Creator /_____\ King
   (Life)              (Liberty)

             GOD
```

The triune nature of God is Creator, Father, King. He is the source of all that is good—life, love, and liberty. This is the the first ancient key, the foundation and root system upon which we can now understand another piece of the secret, another ancient key.

The Good Kingdom

Kings reign over kingdoms. "Everything in heaven and earth is Yours. Yours, Lord, is the kingdom . . . you are the ruler of all things" (1 Chron.

29:11–12). Why is there so much suffering and injustice if God is good and rules over everything? Because he is a good King offering both liberty and mercy. The wise do his will because they know it is right and that by it they will thrive. But some people rebel and do what is in opposition to his will. The king is still lord over all, but his good intentions are not in effect everywhere because he grants his people freedom to choose.

God's kingdom is *now*. It has been there from the beginning because God has been King from the beginning. But it's not being expressed everywhere. That's why when Jesus enjoined us to pray "Your kingdom come" he clarified by adding, "Your will be done on earth as in heaven." We are to pray—which includes putting feet to our prayers—that his will be done in every place where it currently is not being done. When we dare listen to Jesus instead of our preconceived ideas, we realize God is bigger and better than we have realized! God's kingdom is expressed "where what God wants done is done."[8]

The first and paramount way the kingdom comes on earth is through individual people choosing to enter it (become citizens), as we'll see in the next chapter. But because ever since creation God's kingdom is no longer limited to spiritual things, it influences the physical realm as well. Without citizens there is no kingdom. But without the expectation that the citizens will influence a territory, the kingdom cannot express itself. And to the degree that the kingdom is not expressed and demonstrated in some tangible way, fewer people become citizens!

Some characteristics of God's kingdom are "righteousness, peace and joy in the Holy Spirit" (Rom. 14:17). Wherever people embrace God's presence through faith and live in a way that reflects what is good, promoting life, true love, and liberty with responsibility, there his kingdom is expressed. On the other hand, to the degree that there is lostness, destruction, oppression, or poverty, his kingdom is not being expressed because his will is not being done. All who love righteousness should be drawn toward some dark or broken demography, geography or ideology, because we know his heart is crying for the people bound therein. He wants his kingdom to be expressed everywhere!

Jesus' parables use illustrations of salt, leaven, seed, and talents to depict the kingdom. He also alludes to the kingdom in his teachings on light. Each of these finds its efficacy only in its influence on something natural and tangible, something out there in real life. None of these elements finds its purpose only in the internal, the spiritual, or the afterlife. The kingdom of God is intended to influence the King's creation, both spiritual and material. There he desires to plant the seed of faith that inherits salvation, the honesty that chokes out corruption, the leaven of hope that quells the addict's craving, the light of salvation illumining imprisoned hearts, the talent that multiplies, replacing poverty with sufficiency.

> God's kingdom exists wherever God's will is done, wherever his presence is embraced and his goodness showcased.

In Gen. 1 and 2 God's kingdom was fully present not only in the spiritual realm. It was also now being expressed on earth. The Garden of Eden specifically was his kingdom fully expressed in the physical realm, a heaven-on-Earth where no evil was intended to enter. There was no pain or death. God's treasured human beings, the man and the woman, formed the first physical family. They loved, obeyed, and communed with God and loved each other. Infused and enlivened by the radiance of the good Father-Creator-King, all life reflected his goodness and flourished.

"Worship" in that environment didn't look like what we think of worship today. Everything was in alignment with God's goodness; therefore, all that happened in every moment of life constituted worship (Psalm 96:11–12).

Our English translations render the Hebrew *shalom*[9] and Greek *eirene*[10] merely as "peace," the absence of anxiety or war. However, this is a shrunken interpretation. Shalom "describes a whole or fully satisfied situation."[11] It is "wholeness and harmony in relationship with God," "the gift of precious well-being . . . the establishment of a lasting, righteous, good."[12] It is "a condition in which everyone and everything is in right relationship all the time,"[13] or "the way things ought to be."[14] Likewise, *eirene* can mean not just peace but wholeness, a thriving of the person spiritually, physically and emotionally. Where God's kingdom is both entered and expressed, there is Shalom.

The kingdom which had until then existed only in heaven, in the spiritual realm, now was also expressed by matter—flora and fauna, the Father's love displayed through his magnificent handiwork. The blossoming trees, the rushing rivers, the rising and setting sun, the animals in all their vast varieties—all fulfilled his will. All reflected his goodness, one grand orchestra of worship.

But our good Father-Scientist-King's most awesome act of love, art, and splendor was yet to be unveiled . . . The secret of YOUR long-hidden destiny!

2

YOUR TRIUNE ROYALTY

"Let us make mankind in Our image, according to Our likeness; and let them rule . . . over all the earth."

—Gen. 1:26 (NASB)

"The dream of God over your life is that you come alive in his presence and bring life to every environment, spilling contagious hope into hurting humanity. God has entrusted believers with an assignment to lead the earth into life."

—Alan Scott

"Run! Faster!" Ricky urged her two friends onward. The facility where they had barely survived for the past three years due to neglect now lay behind them. They had escaped without being noticed. But if the dogs barked, they would be caught. Fear gripped the girls' hearts as they approached the bend in the road where dogs always lay in wait for anyone passing by. But the time was two in the morning, and to the girls' relief, the dogs were fast asleep. Now another dread filled their hearts: traffickers! Three young girls out alone at night were prime targets for the cruel evil that lurked in the dark.

"The bus stop is near," panted one of the girls. "The bus will take us to the good people who cared for us before."

"How can we ride the bus?" asked her friend. "We have no money."

Ricky spied nearby a dilapidated shed once used to shelter animals. "Let's hide inside this," she said. "No one will find us here. We will be safe. Then when daylight comes we'll try to get on the bus."

Born into extreme poverty, Ricky's father passed away when she was very young. Deprived of a chance to ever know the love of a human father, she was placed in a children's home at age five, then taken to another institution. There she did not receive proper care and could barely survive. When she was eight years old, she and two of her friends escaped and set out to reach the children's home where she had been treated well. Though they could have easily been abducted and trafficked during their harrowing journey, the girls arrived safely.

But good food and education still do not fill a person's need for God and for identity. In the following years Ricky heard the gospel and chose to follow Jesus. Joy filled her life as she grew in her faith and discovered God as her loving father. But for Ricky, that was only the beginning. She also realized God had created her special for a great and unique purpose. Still fresh in her mind were the torment of hunger, fear, and neglect. So she said in her heart, "one day I will rescue other children out of desperate and impoverished situations."

Today Ricky's vision is a reality. Through WIN's children's home, for the last fifteen years Ricky has raised thirty-three beautiful children who were orphans or semi-orphans suffering hunger, abuse, and neglect. These kids are now completing high school and college, and are becoming amazing young leaders. Ricky also is raising two children of her own and manages our vibrant and growing Blue Haven School, providing a top-quality education to hundreds of kids.

Ricky was able to overcome a difficult childhood and fulfill her purpose because she found two powerful keys: She received the love of her father God, and she discovered her incredible identity and mission. You're about to find your identity and mission as well. The forces of darkness fear that you will apprehend this ancient key: the fullness of *who* you are!

Much of the wounding in our world today is the result of our blindness to God's goodness and to our own magnificent calling. Believers are not exempt; our calling has continued to be secret, unrealized, and unfulfilled because we are inhibited by our partial or skewed understanding of the Bible's big picture. The previous chapter disclosed the first set of keys: God as good Father, Creator, and King, author of life, love, and liberty. When we add to this the next set of keys, we will experience an acceleration of abundant life, victorious purpose, and global influence! Let us continue to allow the Bible to unshrink us.

Imago Dei

With the creation of planets, plants, and animals, the Father's handiwork was still incomplete. God "formed a man from the dust of the ground" (Gen. 2:7). Adam comes from *adamah,* meaning "earth." Physical things are not subordinate or of lesser value, for his highest creation was formed from its most humble matter! But humans are not only flesh like animals; neither are we only spirit. God is triune Father, Son, and Spirit, yet these three Persons exist in perfect oneness, the first "family." Likewise, our Father created humans triune—body, soul, and spirit wrapped into one incredible being.

Our good Father gave us a spirit by which to love him and perceive the spiritual realm. He gave us a mind by which to reason, create, and protect. He also gave us five senses by which to experience the physical world—sight, smell, taste, hearing, and touch. All these gifts are so that we may enjoy every aspect of life. No one aspect is to be devalued, but rather our "whole spirit, soul and body" (1 Thess. 5:23) celebrates together the life we've been given by our loving Father, our wise Creator.

When God made physical flora and fauna, it was "good." But now a being had been created which was both flesh and spirit together. Earth's bounty having been completed by the addition of humans, God looked across all as a whole and found "good" to be insufficient. Now this grand symphony of matter and intellect, of physical and spiritual dancing in synchrony and in celebration of life, crowned by God's most intricate handiwork of all, was no longer just "good." Now it was "very good!" (Gen. 1:31).

> Human beings were created to embody God's "very good," celebrating and multiplying love, life and liberty.

Why was creation not declared "very good" until the addition of human beings? Here lies another ancient key!

When we consider that God is a good King and that the earth is intended to showcase his goodness, then it follows that humans have a special calling as the King's royal stewards of his earthy domain. We have three glorious purposes, each of which reflects God's image.

Relationship: Sonship and Family

When God created trees, toads, turkeys, and trout, these were only earthly, for he said, "Let the land produce vegetation" (Gen. 1:11) and "Let the land produce" animals (Gen. 1:24). But human beings are personally and lovingly fashioned from the very hands of God, created "in his own image" (Gen. 1:27). "To glorify God and enjoy Him forever" is the first purpose of human beings and the first aspect in which we are made "*imago dei.*"[1] (Deut. 6:5; Matt. 22:37–40).

Have you ever seen a monkey praying or bowing down to a deity or religious icon? Never. But go to the most remote tribe of humans, even those having had no contact with the outside world, and you will find them worshiping something. They may do obeisance to the sun, or a tree, or a rock, but it's their desperate outlet for the cry for connection with their Maker. Truly did St. Augustine observe, "you have made us for yourself, O Lord, and our hearts are restless until they rest in you."

At age fifteen, I was as far from God as Earth is from Saturn! My gods had four legs that whinnied. I was obsessed with horses—grooming, feeding, cleaning paddocks, studying horse books, and riding, riding, riding, practicing the art of dressage. All this I performed with one fixation: at the next horse show I must move my score up a few points, blitz my peers, and bag the year-end championship. But in all my frenzied pursuit of trophies, joy found no place in my heart. I was mean, argumentative, rebellious, and full of strife.

Then I encountered Jesus. What God allowed me to experience was neither a vision nor a dream. It was as real as real can be. I saw Jesus, spoke with him, and touched him.[2] In that heavenly, holy, and indescribable moment, I knew that God exists, the result of sin is death, and Jesus had suffered its penalty so that I—and every person who puts their trust in him—could be restored into a relationship with God. After a dramatic repentance, I felt so changed on the inside, I was terrified to look in the mirror. It was as if I had become a whole new creature. Indeed, purified of sin, my dormant spirit had been enlivened and indwelt by the Holy Spirit. I had become a daughter of the King of kings, a citizen of God's spiritual kingdom, "born again" into "a new life" (John 3:3; Rom. 6:4). From that moment, everything changed! Though I still enjoyed horses, they were no longer the center of my world. Getting to know Jesus more and more was now my passion. Realizing that my angry thoughts, foul mouth, and selfish actions hurt and displeased him, I waged war on these vices and eventually formed new habits that reflected God's goodness. In place of strife, now joy, peace, and newfound purpose were mine.

Humans are uniquely made for a faith-based relationship with our Father-King. We're not just servants, not even just his children, but princes and princesses, entrusted and authorized heirs.

Being in our very makeup a family—spirit, soul and body, and thus imaging the divine "family" Father, Son and Spirit, it follows that he would commission us to "be fruitful and multiply" (Gen. 1:28 NASB). Because every human has an eternal spirit, procreation is holy. Every child conceived in the womb is, from that moment onward, the very image and likeness of God.

> Salvation unshrunk means adoption into our heavenly Father's royal family and citizenship in his kingdom of life.

This personal experience of relationship with God, which we call salvation, is the starting point but not the whole picture. Like a grand tree spreading upward on a strong and deep root system, upon this essential base rises the rest of our purpose.

There are two further incredible ways by which human beings are to steward and order God's kingdom on earth.

"The LORD God took the man and put him in the Garden of Eden to work it and take care of it" (Gen. 2:15). "Work" and "take care of" sound virtually synonymous. We picture Adam as Eden's gardener, pulling weeds out of the petunias and watering the saplings. But there were no weeds to pull because "thorns and thistles" only came about after humans chose to sin (Gen. 3:18). And there was no need to irrigate, for a mist watered everything (Gen. 2:6). What then does this passage mean? When taken in context with the injunction to rule and subdue, and to multiply and fill (Gen. 1:26–28), this "creation mandate" has monumental connotations. Here lie more ancient keys, secrets that can unleash our glorious potential!

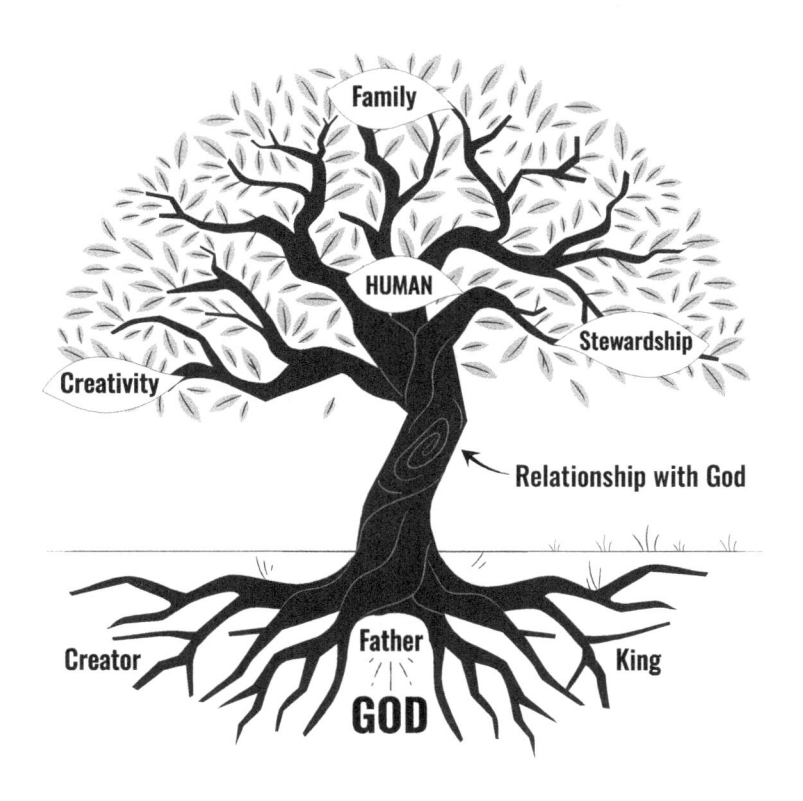

The previous diagram observed that God is Father, Creator and King, the root system and foundation of everything good. Dynamically connected with him by the "trunk" of faith-based relationship, humans reflect his triune image through family (mentioned above), creativity, and stewardship.

Creativity: Art, Science, and Technology

Sadly our diminished view of God and ourselves has left many confused as to where faith and human industry intersect. But the ancient keys you're receiving reveal a glorious synergy! The Hebrew word for "work" or "tend" is *abad*. In Gen. 2:15 "to work" means to "cultivate," "enrich," or "advance." The Creator is the first scientist, originator, and architect of all things. Humans aren't slaves or hired laborers, but trusted and authorized co-creators equipped with a powerful mind. Therefore, "work . . . the garden" also adjures us to "improve upon," "promote the development of," and "refine" all that pertains to the habitat into which he has placed us.

When we cultivate as he intends, we become contributors to his creation. The outcome is all the vast diversity of human culture. Art, engineering, architecture, pharmacology, astronomy—all are intended to reflect God's goodness.

> We express the image of the Creator when from wood we cultivate violins, from stone, houses, from rubber, wheels, and from minerals, microchips.

Abad is the root of *avodah*, a word used interchangeably throughout the Old Testament for both "work" and "worship." When we "tend" and "serve" in an attitude of love toward God and our fellow human beings, and in celebration of his goodness, our cultivating of earth becomes an act of worship.

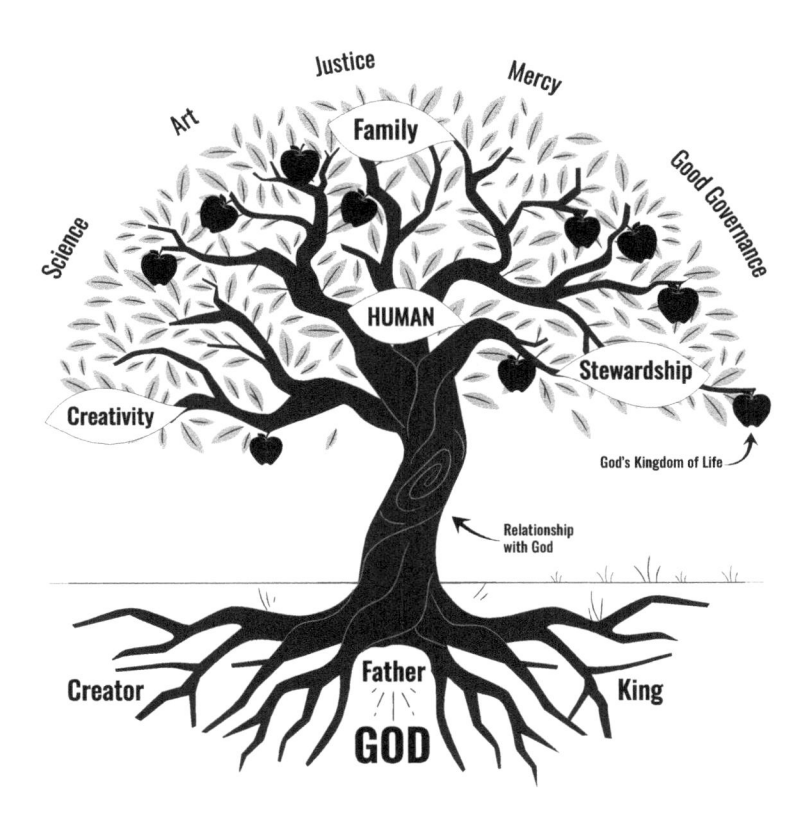

To the degree that humans live in vibrant relationship with the Source of good, to that degree we reflect and multiply his goodness. To the degree that we embrace his principles of true love, life and liberty, to that degree, we produce and achieve good things: the world is filled with the wholesome fruit of cultural beauty, scientific advances, and good governance.

Guardianship: Stewardship and Governance

In any kingdom, the birth of a prince or princess is extremely important. It ensures the kingdom's future leadership. Royal children inherit their father's kingdom. Under the king's supreme authority, we are to administrate the kingdom's many sectors and regions on earth.

Therefore, humans are to "subdue [the earth]; and rule over . . . every living thing" (Gen. 1:28 NASB).

To "rule over" is best understood as "to be a good steward of" and "protect." A steward doesn't make the rules but carries out what the owner determines. We are equipped to administrate our King's good will, ambassadors who facilitate his kingdom to come and his will to be done on earth (Matt. 6:10). The goodness that he embodies, creates, and wills is meant to be expressed on earth.

Every kingdom has enemies. Some threats come from within in the form of bad leadership or corruption. Other threats are external, such as militant regimes desiring to attack and conquer, robbing the people of their freedoms.

That is why Adam and Eve, the first citizens of God's kingdom on earth, had a further task. It was not enough for them to be in relationship with their Father and with each other. Neither was it enough that they create along with the Creator by cultivating his raw materials. Adam was to both work and "take care of" the garden. The Hebrew word *shawmehr* is often translated "keep" and means "to keep watch, to guard." If you're charged with the task of guarding something, it follows that there is an enemy who wants to corrupt or steal it!

"Now the serpent was more crafty than any of the wild animals" (Gen. 3:1). Satan, a rebellious angel (Ezek. 28), desired to enslave the human race and the whole earth. Hater of all things good, he schemed to destroy God's beloved human beings and his "very good" kingdom of heaven on earth. This could only occur if earth's appointed stewards were separated from relationship with God, the source of life. If they sinned by failing to "keep guard" of their hearts and of creation, then death could take over.

This is why God's command was not just to fill the earth but to "subdue it." Guardianship involves subduing our desires that are not in alignment with God's good will, and also subduing the demonic realm, the powers that corrupt and promote all manifestations of death. Sin, therefore, is failed guardianship.

The original intent was not merely for Adam and Eve to live happily ever after within the limited boundaries of the garden that God had planted for them. Eden was intended to be only a starting point, a pattern. Human beings were to expand this paradise, the physical manifestation of God's heavenly kingdom, throughout the entire earth. They were to fill the earth not just with more human beings, but with human beings who walked and talked with God in a vibrant joyous relationship, loving each other, building families, and living according to God's goodness. People who worshiped him by being co-creators, turning his raw materials into good things, and who guarded and stewarded the earth protecting it from evil. This is the full meaning of the assignment to be fruitful and multiply and fill the earth.

> As a good king protects his territory, humans are to be guardians of our Father-King's world, protecting life, celebrating true love and promoting responsible liberty.

Humans are unique and precious beyond all imagination. "Consider how precious a soul must be," observed Charles Spurgeon, "when both God and the devil are after it." This is why first and foremost our eternal salvation and secondly our earthly stewardship are important.

You're seeing a preliminary glimpse of your secret calling—the awesome triune importance that you as a human "fearfully and wonderfully made" in God's image, occupy in the cosmos (Psalm 139:14)!

But then these keys, this foundational glimpse of our secret calling was stolen, corrupted, and lost . . .

3

A WOUNDED WORLD

"Cursed is the ground because of you; through painful toil you will eat food from it all the days of your life.
—Gen. 3:17

"We should not ask, "What is wrong with the world?" for that diagnosis has already been given. Rather, we should ask, "Where is the salt and light? Where is the Church? Why are the salt and light of Jesus Christ not permeating and changing our society?"
—John Stott

"The Bible taught that the Creator did not intend life to be suffering. God created Adam and Eve to live in Eden—in bliss. Suffering came later, as a result of sin. Suffering is thus a historical fact, not a metaphysical truism—which means it can and should be resisted."
—Vishal Mangalwadi

2018: Banal Banshan

"We can't eat today," Yulan murmured. "We must go hungry today and eat tomorrow." Her tear-filled eyes gazed hopelessly into the rice bag. Only one more meal's worth of the precious grains remained. She cast a disgusted glance toward the only other room of their mud hut. Inside, heavy snores emanated from the rickety string-and-wood cot. Her husband had been out drinking last night. The money that should have bought rice had been wasted on liquor—again.

Outside a girl of about nine with sun-bleached matted hair and dull eyes squatted near a buffalo, gathering its dried dung into a reed basket—fuel for a fire that would satiate their empty stomachs with nothing but black tea. A stone's throw away beneath a bamboo cluster stood a naked toddler with a bloated belly. His grimy fingers gripped a piece of sugarcane, the other end of which he mouthed.

On a dirt path winding between the huts and buffalo herd ambled three men.

Wedging the basket under one arm, the girl took her little brother by the hand. Casting wary glances at the newcomers, the two children made their way to their hut.

Stooping, Yulan peered out under the hut's four-foot-high rough wood lintel past a dangling protrusion of rotting thatch. She observed that the men wore shoes, not just flip-flops. Their trousers had no holes, and their shirts weren't so threadbare as to have lost their original color. That meant the men were either outsiders or from the family of the chief. In this case, they were both.

From the necks of two of the men bobbed ID badges. Rural development officers had been dispatched to assess the status of the village. One of them sidestepped human excrement only to have his foot roll on one of many Pabst Blue Ribbon and Tsingtao bottles littering the edge of the path. With a disgusted face he declared, "Sir, your village is in a despicable state, but there is no excuse for such backwardness. This location isn't too far from the city. Residents who don't own fields can commute and find employment. So, why the extreme poverty and filth?"

"Ma!" Inside the hut, the girl coughed explosively as she tugged at her mother's dress. "Ma, I don't feel good." In the other room the toddler had fallen and was screaming.

"Ah Lam, go tend to your brother!" Yulan snapped, and remained there in the doorway to eavesdrop on the conversation outside.

The village chief maintained a strict poker face, walking stick keeping time with his slightly lame right leg. "My people are fools," he barked. "They have neither self-control nor a desire to improve themselves. In nearly every home, the devil rules through the curse of drunkenness."

The mother glared at the chief. Just silent enough that the men couldn't hear, she spit, "Hypocrite! You yourself are making things worse!" Last year she had asked him to provide some kind of counseling or program to help the husbands—who composed 90 percent of the alcoholics—get free from the devilish addiction. But instead, when the time came for the local election, he had provided free alcohol!

The men halted as the other officer opened a booklet. "Sir, training is available on health and hygiene and the dangers of poor sanitation. But there is still human excrement in the ditches and the fields."

"The people don't care," protested the chief. "They say, why waste good fertilizer?"

"Do they know they will get parasites and all sorts of sicknesses? Do they know only animal dung should be used on the crops?" queried the officer. "If they are not aware of basic hygiene, then it is your responsibility to arrange for them to be educated."

The response offered by the chief was to extract a packet of tobacco, empty it into his mouth, and flick the plastic into the ditch.

Shaking his head, the officer with the booklet took a pen from his pocket and began to write. "Sir, I regret to say that based on our observations, your village is sorely underdeveloped. A large percentage of the children aren't in school, toddlers are malnourished, almost everyone we met was sick, and every family except yours is in extreme poverty. I have to report Banshan as one of the most banal communities in our district."

Poverty, addictions, and slavery were never God's will. God is Light and Life, but these are expressions of death. They are manifestations of the corruption that have victimized his good creation through us humans misusing our freedom.

The Sin Pandemic

Human beings were intended to subdue the Serpent's evil intent. We were not merely to keep him from corrupting the garden of God's perfect kingdom on Earth; we were to expand Eden into the rest of the planet. But Adam failed to keep watch, to guard the garden, therefore the Serpent gained access to Eden. Adam then neglected to also protect his wife. Eve forthwith failed to keep guard of the garden of her heart. They both chose to do evil. Their relationship with God was severed. Instead of God's love-sourced kingdom of life, they chose to align themselves with the kingdom of destruction presided by Satan, "ruler of the kingdom of the air," the devil who "has been sinning from the beginning" (Eph. 2:2; 1 John 3:8). When the first man and woman were driven out of

Eden, it symbolized the severing of their life-giving relationship with God. The prince and princess had removed themselves from the King's family. The stewards of the kingdom of God on earth were now slaves of an illegitimate and cruel master—the false prince the devil—and his kingdom of death (John 8:34–36).

Because God is the author of life, separation from him means death—spiritual death and physical death in all its manifestations. So now humans would suffer pain and death. Now the earth would bring forth thorns and thistles, for earth's authorized stewards, tasked with administration of God's kingdom on earth, had conveyed it to the destroyer. "Every manifestation of evil is the result of basic sin."[1] The essential basis of the kingdom of God on earth—relationship between humans and God—had been severed.

Sin is the first pandemic and the originator of all other pandemics—death, corruption, plagues, oppression, human trafficking, war. Like the opening of Pandora's Box, sin released a pandemic both spiritual and physical upon God's good creation. Creation did not become evil. It became a victim. Physical things and life itself were still good, but because the King's stewards had chosen not to align with his truth and goodness, all that they administrated now suffered "bondage to decay" (Rom. 8:21).

A WOUNDED WORLD

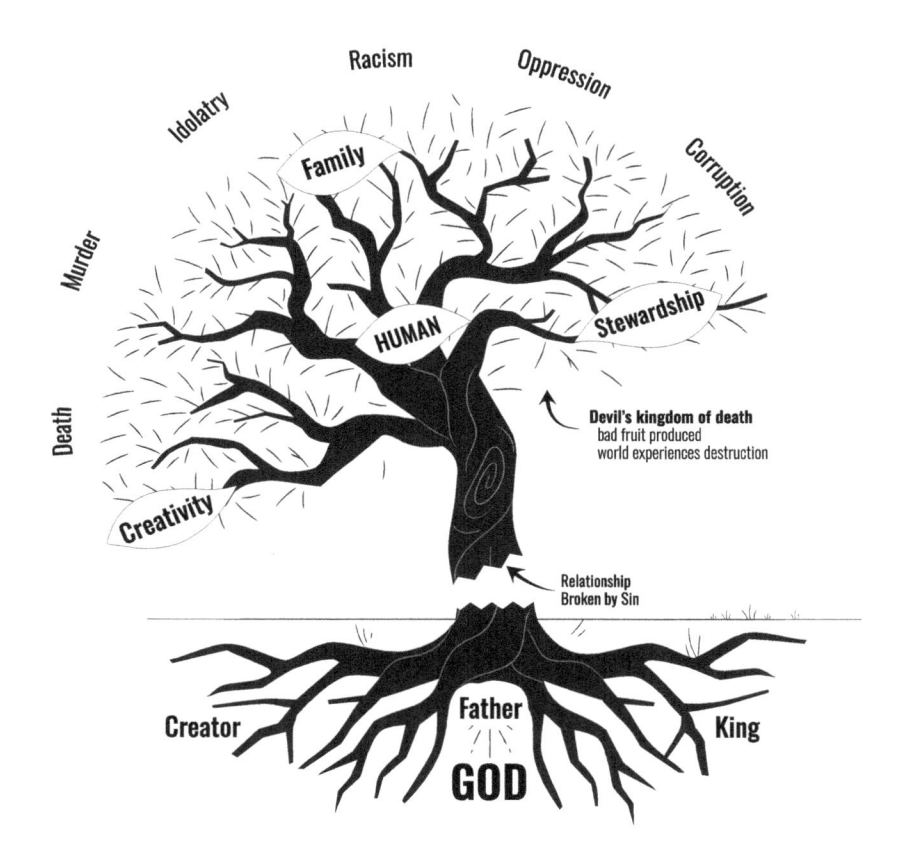

Sin severed the relationship between humans and God. God's kingdom on earth came into the governance of the enemy. Death came upon all things. To the degree that humans depart from God's life-giving principles, we also misuse our creativity and stewardship, producing the harmful fruits of idolatry, racism, murder, and oppression.

Yet all was not lost. There was still hope.

The Healing Foreshadowed

God did not abandon his beloved human beings nor his earth. The broken relationship would be healed, his good kingdom on earth restored. But death must occur in order to heal the death pandemic. As the blood of some furry animals drained out in order to provide skins to clothe them, Adam and Eve witnessed the terrible price of sin (Gen. 3:21). The first blood sacrifice had been made, the first symbolic act of healing the broken relationship. This constitutes the first prophesy of Jesus by whose shed blood our loving Father would bring about the true healing many years later.

Jesus was again foreshadowed when the lamb's blood on the doorposts of the Hebrew homes ensured that death would pass over their firstborn (Exod. 12:13). Thus, Jesus is called our Passover lamb (1 Cor. 5:7), slain so that His blood, the healing "balm of Gilead" placed upon the doorposts of our hearts by faith, "heals" us from eternal death (Jer. 8:22), ensuring that "whoever believes in him shall not perish but have eternal life" (John 3:16).

While this is the foundation, it's not the whole building. While this is the tree trunk, it's not the whole tree. Our diminished partial understanding has us spend our whole lives in this same place, saved, satisfied, but not delving further, never discovering our secret calling.

Crushing the Serpent's Head

When Satan said to Eve, "You will not certainly die," he lied (Gen. 3:4). The consequence of aligning with the enemy by disobeying God was death (Gen. 2:17; Rom. 6:23). Adam and Eve's sin severed humans from their relationship with the source of all life, bringing about spiritual death and material corruption. But a few verses later, our loving Father God, in his great mercy, uttered a glorious promise: The "seed" of the woman would one day crush the evil one's head (Gen. 3:15 NKJV). In natural conception, the man contributes the seed, i.e., the sperm, while the woman contributes the ovum. So what is meant by the "seed" of the woman? Right here in the third chapter of Genesis, the virgin birth of

Jesus is foreshadowed. The coming Deliverer, conceived by a miraculous act of God through a woman who had never had sexual relations with a man, would win freedom not just for a part of creation but for the whole of it. As King of all and as Creator of life, he would crush the prince of death and reinitiate God's kingdom on earth.

What happens when ordinary people live out their secret calling and, through the victory of Christ, crush the head of lostness, corruption, and poverty? What happens when God unleashes his highest purpose through you? Broken people are turned into champions. Hopelessness is transformed into victory.

Back to Banshan

"Hello, is anyone home?" Yulan's woes were interrupted by a female voice, which she knew by the inflection wasn't of a local woman.

She ducked outside, and the women exchanged the traditional greeting. Sujia and her teammate introduced themselves as part of the nonprofit organization We Ignite Nations (WIN).[2] They had come to see if WIN could help Banshan.

Yulan's hut was too small to accommodate guests, so she dragged out the only available piece of furniture—a second cot—and bid them sit. According to the culture, a host too impoverished to serve a guest milk tea and biscuits nevertheless offers water and sugar. So hurrying back inside, from a plastic bucket drawn from the local well earlier that morning, Yulan filled steel cups. Then for a long moment she stared at her sugar urn. It contained only a few spoonfuls of the costly white granules that would provide the little pleasure in their palate. With a sigh she emptied it into a small steel bowl and searched for her sole piece of silverware, a spoon. A steel plate, still wet from its scrubbing with mud since dish soap was an unimaginable luxury, doubled for a serving tray.

"Tell us about your family," Sujia urged. Seating herself on the other end of the cot, Yulan poured out her troubles. Her husband was a drunkard, and her family often went hungry. Pointing to a scar, she told of the last time he had hit her in a drunken rage. She knew her daughter should be in school, but she instead had to work or care for her brother. Her children were always sick. By the end of her story, Yulan was sobbing. Sujia's teammate put a comforting arm around her shoulders.

"Those buffaloes—are they yours?"

"No. We are just allowed to gather their dung."

"Do you have a field of your own?" asked Sujia.

"No," sniffled Yulan. "We have no field."

"See this land right here around your hut? Would you like to learn how to grow vegetables—not enough to sell, but for you and your family to eat?"

Yulan looked puzzled, but nodded.

"If there were a program in your village to help people get free of alcoholism, do you think your husband would participate?" asked Sujia.

"I don't know," Yulan muttered. "Maybe he would."

About then, Yulan's husband Nanyou emerged from the hut. His cheeks and eyes were sunken, and his thin frame reeked of alcohol. Sujia and her teammate rose and greeted him and Nanyou carried the other cot outside so there was more space to sit.

After small talk, Sujia asked Nanyou to tell about his family, his job, his village.

"I'm so frustrated," mourned Nanyou. "No matter how hard I work, I don't feel like I can ever provide enough for my family. I hate myself. Most of us here in this village feel the same way. Whenever the paycheck comes, I go and drown my sorrows with liquor. I know that's foolish, but

I can't stop. I don't know what to do."

Sujia and her teammate smiled at each other, because they could see that this family was willing to be guided into the biblical principles that could change their lives for the better.

⋄ ⋅⋅ ⋄

On the other side of Banshan at the home of the village chief, WIN leader Haomu and his teammate had been joined by the local pastor. Reclining in plastic chairs, they dipped a second helping of biscuits into the strong tea proudly proffered by the chief's wife. Brow furrowed with perplexity, the chief asked for the third time, "So you people aren't offering any aid to my village? No bags of rice? No money, not even loans?"

"We are offering to teach your people how to grow their own nutritious food and how to earn and save their own money," said Haomu. "Outside aid gives them food for a month, but what happens when that runs out?"

"They are hungry again," admitted the chief. "But they don't want to change."

"Sometimes," said the pastor, "when people realize that they are valuable and that there is hope for a better future, they are able to dream again. Then they have the inner strength to make the right choices."

"I know you all are Christians," said the chief. "Others have come here offering charity and programs, but all they wanted was to preach to us. So what do you really want?"

The pastor opened his Bible. "Sir, we want for Banshan what God wants. Do you know what God wants for you and your village?"

The chief shrugged.

The pastor handed the Bible to him and pointed to a passage. "Please read this."

When the chief had finished reading Deuteronomy 28:2–6, the pastor said, "That is what God wants for Banshan! He wants to bless you and your community in every way. And that is also what we want."

"We are offering to provide training for the people so their lives can improve," said Haomu. "But we will not do anything unless you endorse it. Our goal is that every household will participate. Many of the people will be asked to volunteer their time by training and coaching others."

Two fingers disappeared into his shirt pocket and reappeared with the usual packet of chewing tobacco. "I don't mind you trying. I'm happy to endorse your efforts. But don't get your hopes up. These people are stubborn as buffaloes.

"No problem," Haomu reassured him. "What we ask of you is two things. In the first meeting, will you come and speak to the people and encourage them to participate?"

Encumbered to reply due to his mouthful of snuff, the chief wagged his head sideways, meaning "yeah, sure."

"Also, would you recommend five people from this village whom you feel should be on the Committee?"

With that, the chief's brows went up. He could put his buddies in these roles. Having only begun to enjoy his snuff, he spat most of it into the weeds so he could talk. "Local Committee? You mean you all aren't going to lead this?"

"Only from behind," said the pastor. "We'll provide coaching, but this will be your project. You are going to be the champions!"

"You're suggesting a different kind of project than others who came here," admitted the chief. "Certainly! I will recommend Committee members. When do we start?"

Six Months Later: Booming Banshan

"Don't be late for school!" Yulan shouted to Ah Lam. "But first come get your breakfast." Perched on a low stool, Yulan's bare toes anchored a knife on which she sliced a squash into chunks. A contented smile spread her cheeks.

Fiddling with her belt and followed by her brother, Ah Lam darted from the bedroom. Her once-sad face was now full of color and life. Savoring a bowl of porridge and a hard-boiled egg, she could hardly remember the former days of stomach pain and sickness. While her daughter ate, Yulan buckled her belt, straightened her spiffy school dress, and fixed her hair in two cute braids with blue bows. Then she hefted chubby Bao Bei onto her knee and began feeding him porridge.

"Do you want your children to suffer like you have been suffering?" the WIN team had asked.

"No!" cried the parents.

"Educate your children now, and when they grow up, they will not be poor." The team had worked with the parents to help them find ways to ensure their children could go to school. Some had to figure out transportation. Others had to work harder themselves, so the child's labor was no longer needed.

As one of the first to sign up to be a Champion, today Yulan would make her house calls. With the evening meal prepared in advance, she would have plenty of time to do what had come to be her favorite part of the week.

After Ah Lam joined the other children on their walk to the nearby school, Yulan washed the dishes with soap and set aside boiled water to cool for future drinking. Then she dressed Bao Bei in the first new piece of clothing the family had bought in years: bright blue trousers and a yellow shirt printed with a choo choo train. Yulan donned the second piece of new clothing in the home: a pretty red-and-pink dress purchased from a discount store.

She took a quick assessment of her "kitchen garden." Squash hung from the vines, peas bulged their pods, and beans dangled from trellises. There were also cabbages, carrots, tomatoes, and turnips. Her family had never eaten such nutritious food in their lives! The WIN team had taught her the importance of nutrition and how to cultivate every inch of ground available. She had never imagined so much food could be produced within a few yards of her hut.

"Be generous to your neighbors," the WIN team had taught. "God's Book tells us, 'Give and it will be given to you.'" So Yulan plucked a meal's supply of beans, picked up her WIN Champions satchel, and took Bao Bei by the hand. They walked a few huts over to her neighbor, her first visit of the day.

Daiyu was milking a goat.

"You didn't used to have any animals," observed Yulan.

"We just got her!" Daiyu beamed. "Remember last month when the WIN trainers taught us that we don't have to give money to the witch doctor? It only took a few weeks of saving that money. Now I have fresh milk and a baby goat too!"

Daiyu received the beans with great appreciation since her garden hadn't fared as well as Yulan's. "Tell me how you're caring for your garden," said Yulan. But as soon as she saw the garden, she knew the problem: Daiyu was letting the weeds grow up and smother the plants. Yulan moved on to her next appointment, leaving a thankful Daiyu extracting weeds and piling them into a mound to be fed to her goat.

With a deep sense of satisfaction Yulan returned to her hut after completing her route. Nanyou had arrived from work. Strapped over the rear wheel of his bicycle was a big bag of rice and on top of it another bag of flour and on top of that a third bag of soybeans. "Here's all the things you can't grow in the garden," he said with pride. He no longer smelled of alcohol, only of the sweat of a good day's labor. "And because I stopped drinking and being late, my boss gave me a raise!"

The family celebrated as they enjoyed an ample dinner of rice, beans, and vegetables seasoned with delectable spices.

After some time, the Committee and WIN's trainers took a survey to assess the progress. Almost every family had experienced some significant improvement in health, happiness, and living standard. Alcoholism had all but disappeared. The bottle-littered paths had been cleaned up, and muddy paths had been paved with bricks. Most of the families now had "kitchen gardens," and malnutrition had all but been eradicated. Children were now going to school, and illness had been more than halved. Curious about what motivated the WIN team and where these life-transforming principles came from, many began attending Bible classes taught by the pastor and his disciples.

Now the trainers were ready to take the people of Banshan to the next step: saving their money and then using it to build homes of brick instead of mud.

The development officer hesitated outside Yulan's home. He ogled about in bewilderment and double-checked the coordinates in his record book.

His companion had never visited Banshan before. "What's wrong?" he asked.

"I think we're in the wrong place," said the senior. "But when I came here two years ago, I swear we traversed the very same roads."

Yulan saw them. "Hello!" she shouted from the doorway of her home. "No worries, you're in the right place."

About fifty feet away, Nanyou and his friend were installing a wooden door on the new bathroom. Nanyou greeted the guests with a grin. "Big change, do you agree?"

The senior officer was incredulous. He couldn't believe it was the same community.

⁂

Banshan became a model of how an ancient key - realignment with our Father-King's life-giving principles - can reverse some element of the sin-death pandemic, replacing destruction with hope. This case study and those coming up next provide glimpses into your secret calling. They are examples by which any individual, church, business, nonprofit, or network can bring healing into the woundedness around us. But there are many more ancient keys to be revealed! Your secret calling will only be unleashed by discovering that Jesus is much more powerful than we ever imagined.

4

UNSHRINKING JESUS

"I have come that they may have life, and have it to the full."
—John 10:10

"Jesus, by his choices of destinations, friends, and subject matter, teaches us how to reach the world. Like him, we must go to the whole world. We cannot skip over the Samaritans because everyone else despises them… We must explode the myths about Jesus in favor of the reality of Jesus."
—Dr. Thomas E. Hatley

Drugs, Suicide, and Crime

"*I*'m going to KILL YOU!"

Mike leaped out of bed as Rennae let out a scream. The deep growling utterance had come from outside the ground-level window of their basement abode. One kick and the glass would shatter. One gunshot through the glass and . . .

"Get out of the room, honey! Get to safety!" Mike urged.

Rennae stood trembling beside the bed. "You come too! He might attack us!"

Flipping on the light, heart in his throat, Mike tried to collect his wits. He had recognized the voice as that of someone who had recently been in trouble for disturbing others in the neighborhood.

Mike felt his hand going to the window. With a swoosh he pulled back the curtain.

The person who had threatened them had fled.

Though the couple breathed a sigh of relief, they also felt the crushing weight of the spiritual darkness. The Lord had called them from comfort in the suburbs to this inner-city area known as Eight Ball Street, so named for the rampant drug addiction that rotted human lives from the inside out. Two other related pandemics were tormenting the troubled town: crime and suicide. How much longer could they persevere in this hopeless place?

Some days later, as Rennae walked through the church parking lot, the man reappeared. Following her, he belted out angry words and grew increasingly agitated.

Rennae about-faced. Looking the man in the eyes, she asked, "Which do you prefer: shall I call the cops, or pray for you in Jesus' name?"

At the name of Jesus, the man began to tremble violently. His eyes rolled back in his head, and with bony fingers he clawed at his matted hair. Then a sound came out of him which wasn't that of a man. A demon spoke through him with a deep, raspy guttural voice. It growled, "I'm fighting against your God!" Then he stumbled away.

※ ·•· ※

The kingdom of evil knows and dreads an ancient mystery that has been veiled to the majority of humans, including Christians: who Jesus really is! When we apprehend this truth and receive his grace and power, the enemy kingdom's rampage against God's beloved image bearers and good creation will be driven back. Wholeness, life, and joy will be released, along with exponential revival.

Christ: The Anointed Deliverer King

Jesus is King and Lord in two dimensions, both declared within the angel's announcement to Mary: as "Son of the Most High," he is fully God, pre-existing creation, bestower of life in all dimensions both earthly and eternal, ruler of all things (Luke 1:32). He would deliver human beings out of the kingdom of darkness, healing the broken relationship with our Father God, restoring us to citizenship in God's kingdom of life.

The passage continues, "The Lord God will give him the throne of his father David . . . his kingdom will never end" (Luke 1:32–33). In order to heal the sin-death pandemic, he had to also become man—Immanuel, "God with us"—the christened One, the Messiah, the Deliverer (Matt. 1:23). Jesus is called "Son of man" (Matt. 9:6) because he embodied everything that Adam was intended to, demonstrating how human beings were to live in purity, love unconditionally, and steward every sector of life.

No, "Christ" is not Jesus' surname! *Christos* (Christ) in Greek and *Mashiach* (Messiah) in Hebrew both mean "anointed." In the Old Testament, priests and especially kings were anointed with oil, symbolizing the presence and power of God's Spirit upon their future administration. Prophets were called and empowered directly by God (Exod. 29:7; 1 Sam. 16:13; 3:8–9).

But Jesus is anointed[1] as all three: Priest (Heb. 4:14–16), Prophet (Deut. 18:15; Acts 7:37), and King (Isa. 9:6–7). When the Holy Spirit declared through Peter, "You are the Christ" (Matt. 16:16), those present would have immediately understood Jesus to be the long-awaited bearer of this triune and therefore complete, all-encompassing divine unction. The Deliverer-King had arrived. As Priest he would save spiritually. As King he would save physically. He would impact all of life, both the tangible and intangible. He would redeem and restore in *all* dimensions, both heavenly and earthly, both present and future.

The coming of this Deliverer-King, the "messianic hope," lay at the core of the Jewish people's theology and civil life. Passages such as "he will bring justice to the nations" (Isa. 42:1) and "I will appoint you . . . as a light to the nations" (Isa. 42:6 NASB) indicated a deliverance that would impact the entire world.

What does Jesus' triune anointing mean for us? It's just one more indication of God's all-embracing goodness.

> Jesus came not to extract a few souls into a segregated, earth-abjuring religious community. He came to "reconcile . . . all things" to the Father through the cross (Col. 1:20).

The spiritual is the basis of thriving in all spheres. When God's people held fast to their faith and lived according to his will, their physical lives experienced peace, abundance, and purpose (Deut. 28). Shalom—whole-person and whole-society thriving—is what God's heavenly kingdom looks like, and that is his will for earth as well. While the full outward expression of this reconciliation and healing will only occur when Jesus returns and makes "all things new," his kingdom is here *now*. He is King, Priest, and Prophet *now*, and he wants to express through us as much of it as possible, resulting in a myriad more precious people joining Peter in the joyful confession, "You are the Christ, the Son of the living God" (Matt. 16:16).

When we apprehend and practice this whole-life redemption, a multiplied deliverance will be released across all that we touch. This is a beginning glimpse of God's highest purpose in which we are gloriously called to participate!

The Cross: The Ransom to Reinitiate the Good Kingdom

Only God King of all, Creator of good, Father of life, could annihilate the death curse, the power of Satan, false prince, and primordial sinner (1 John 3:8). But by human choice the kingdom had been lost, the pandemic released, so by human blood the kingdom must be restored, the pandemic quelled (1 Cor. 15:21–22; Heb. 2:9–18; 10:4). Only a perfect, sinless human being could pay the penalty for the sin of human beings, thus making possible restored relationship. This unique "last Adam" would alone be qualified to heal and restore that which the "first Adam" had surrendered (1 Cor. 15:22, 45). Therefore, "God so loved the world" that he gave Jesus, setting in motion the plan to one day fully heal the sin pandemic and all its consequences (John 3:16).

A king has three things: territory, citizens, and authority. In ancient times, when any of these were threatened, good kings didn't sit behind the lines. Gideon, David, and Jehoshaphat are examples of leaders who went out ahead of their people in battle to protect or to secure their freedoms. When Jesus went to the cross, he went as our King before us into battle. But he didn't do so with a limited human sword nor against a mortal enemy. Some erred by expecting him to merely deliver a single nation from their human oppressors.

However, because he is King of *all*, a mere temporal deliverance was too small. Jesus invaded the source of evil, fighting a war of a higher caliber. He attacked earth's pandemic of sin, authored by the devil. Not only did he confront death itself and vanquish it with life (2 Tim. 1:10); "Having disarmed the powers and authorities, he made a public spectacle of them" (Col. 2:15). Referring to how the Roman military celebrated their victories by stripping defeated foes of their weapons and parading them through the streets, this passage indicates the completeness and finality of Christ's victory over spiritual wickedness.

When we see that Jesus is our Lord and King, we recognize also that the cross followed by the resurrection is far more than a religious or purely other-worldly, next-life transaction. The cross and the resurrection of Christ represent the greatest victory in the history of the cosmos! The King who is above all kings ransomed his captive citizens. He paid the penalty for human sin and made the way for us to be forgiven and thus reunited with Father God. His shed blood heals the source of the sin pandemic, enabling all who put their faith in him to flee the kingdom of death and become naturalized into God's kingdom of life.

> The restored relationship achieved by Jesus on the cross also restored the potential of his kingdom of light to be manifested where formerly the kingdom of darkness held sway.

Our traditions have allowed that to be the end goal. Spiritual salvation, however, is not intended to be the climax but the commencement!

Here's a secret treasure, an ancient key; because of Christ's victory, now wherever any person embraces and practices his life-giving principles such as justice, truthfulness, honor, and forgiveness, some sector of the pandemic's destructive symptoms will be reversed. Wherever believers live as true disciples, demonstrating and proclaiming his good, life-giving kingdom, healing can flow into all of creation and salvation will exponentially increase.

The Resurrection: Life's Victory over the Death Pandemic

When Jesus rose from the dead, he secured eternal life for all who believe (1 Cor. 15:53–54). He didn't become a ghost. He could be physically touched and shared a delectable meal with his disciples (Luke 24:39; John 21:9, 13). Herein lies an ancient and hidden key: Why is the body resurrected? Like Jesus, after passing from this world, we also will have new bodies, not merely spirit bodies like angels. Why?

Because God created our bodies *good* and his end goal is complete restoration, not annihilation (Acts 3:21; Rom. 8:18–25; Col. 1:13). Bodily resurrection indicates that both the spiritual and physical, including this life here on earth, are precious. Human life is so valuable that God brings it back from death, breaking the bonds of Hades. The perishable mortal is clothed with the imperishable and immortal, death swallowed up in victory (1 Cor. 15:53–54).

Note that Jesus' resurrected body was superhuman! He was able to walk through walls and, at the climax, ascended to heaven with neither helicopter nor airplane! This is the stuff of Superman movies, but in our resurrected bodies, it will be real.

Our partial understanding has led us to believe that when Jesus returns, the earth will be completely annihilated, everything incinerated as if created things and human art, science and culture were of no value. This is a dualistic and inaccurate view. Created things will not be utterly destroyed but purified and changed, renewed—in a sense, resurrected.

> The spiritual redemption achieved in Christ's death and resurrection is meant also to purify the physical things of life, resulting in one complete celebration of God's goodness.

All that pertains to life—soul, mind, emotions, and body, God's creation and all the products of human creativity—are intended to be redeemed, realigned into God's perfect plan, and then glorified, made even more beautiful. And it can begin right now!

Salvation: Multidimensional Wholeness

The name *Jesus* is derived from the Hebrew/Aramaic *Yeshua*, meaning "Yaweh (God) saves." The root verb *yasha* means "to deliver" or "to rescue." Jesus was so named because he would "save his people from their sins" (Matt. 1:21). By having "taste[d] death for everyone" (Heb. 2:9) and then rising from the grave, he "destroyed death and has brought life and immortality to light through the gospel" (2 Tim. 1:10). Thus he "[broke] the power of him who holds the power of death—that is, the devil" (Heb. 2:14). The tangible outworking of Jesus having crushed the serpent's head, achieving the victory of life over death, will be brought to full and complete expression in the physical dimension when Jesus, our Deliverer-King returns. "The last enemy to be destroyed is death" (1 Cor. 15:26). When that occurs, "there will be no more death or mourning or crying or pain" (Rev. 21:4).

A word we often use almost synonymously with salvation is atonement. Atonement is the restoration of at-one-ment between God and human beings. Remember the tree that produced good fruit so long as the relationship with God was unbroken. But when at-one-ment was destroyed by human sin, we automatically became slaves of the kingdom of death, separated from our holy Father and giver of life.

> Atonement is the transfer of a person out of the jurisdiction of death and naturalization into God's kingdom of life.

"For he has rescued us from the dominion of darkness and brought us into the kingdom of the Son he loves" (Col. 1:13). Appropriating Jesus' victory and being reunited with God is a matter of faith. "Believe in the Lord Jesus, and you will be saved" (Acts 16:31).

Real faith produces repentance, a turning away from sin and a turning toward God's goodness. The "bridge" message that transitioned the old covenant to the new covenant was proclaimed both by John the Baptist and Jesus: "Repent, for the kingdom of heaven is at hand"(Matt. 3:2; 4:17 NASB).[2] Citizenship in the kingdom of light comes with the expectation that we will no longer intentionally align with darkness. It means walking in the light, as he is in the light (1 John 1:7).

Then comes the rest of our life, in which we live out that "at-one-ment" as a disciple of Christ. Traditionally, this involves studying the Bible, praying, keeping ourselves from sin, participating in a church community, giving of our time, talents, and treasure, and sharing our faith when opportunity arises. All of that is true and essential, but it is partial. It's like enjoying the appetizer and then leaving the table, never realizing the wine, barbeque, veggies, and dessert are still coming!

If we make "Savior" and "atonement" refer only to the cleansing of our sins and readying us for the afterlife, then we are diminishing God's goodness. Yes, Jesus is our High Priest, the sole mediator between God and human beings (1 Tim. 2:5–6). But remember, Jesus is also Prophet and King. He is the Great Physician. His blood is the "medicine" that heals the sin pandemic, and his life demonstrated victory over all its evil symptoms. Now, through those who live as true disciples, he desires to disseminate the same.

Therefore, being "saved" must be permitted to mean a salvation, a redemption, a rescuing, a healing that impacts first our own lives, wherein through the indwelling power of his Holy Spirit we cultivate, through love-sourced self-discipline, a lifestyle of turning away from sin.

Secondly, being "saved" means bringing his goodness into all sectors of human existence, specifically into those where our circumstances, employment, or education has given us influence. "Atonement" means a restored at-one-ment, humans joining God in his highest purpose of restoring us into his family and then bringing goodness and life to bear against every manifestation of death. He saves us into newness, victory, and purpose for life right now as well as life eternal. We are a "new creation. The old has gone" (2 Cor. 5:17). We are now "God's handiwork, created in Christ Jesus" (Eph. 2:10). And for what purpose are we thus re-created? "To do good works" (Eph. 2:10). These "good works" include demonstrating his goodness through responsible stewardship as imagers of the good King. Through strong marriages, families, and discipleship of others, we image our loving Father. And as imagers of the wise Creator, we glorify him through art and creativity.

5

DE-FRAGMENTING THE GOSPEL

"In him was life, and that life was the light of all mankind. . . . The true light that gives light to everyone was coming into the world."
—John 1:4, 9

"I sometimes worry that we have settled for a little gospel, a miniaturized version that cannot address the robust problems of our world."
—Scot McKnight

What exactly is the "gospel"? We would likely reply, "Why, it is forgiveness of sins" or "It is the message of Jesus' death and resurrection to save those who believe and to give us eternal life." This is absolutely and wonderfully true, but incomplete.

The Greatest Victory

Euangelion was a well-known word in the time of Christ. When Rome won a battle, a person called an "evangelist" would be sent to ride or run through the streets shouting, "We won the battle! The empire has expanded! You are part of a world-impacting movement!" Thus, "gospel" meant the good news of a military victory, of the expansion of the Roman empire into new territories.

Secondly, the crowning of an emperor or king—and even that dignitary himself—was described as *euangelion*. A Greek inscription dating just eleven years before Christ's birth reads, "The birthday of the god Augustus was the beginning of the good tidings for the world."[1] The annunciation of Jesus' birth uses the same language because he is, truly, King of all! It declares "good news of great joy which will be for all the people"(Luke 2:10 NASB).

Long before the Greek and Roman Empires, the Hebrew equivalent of *gospel* was *besorah*. One of our most beloved prophesies of Jesus the Deliverer is "How delightful on the mountains are the feet of one who brings good news [*besorah*], who announces peace, and brings good news [*besorah*] of happiness" (Isa. 52:7 NASB).

In the Hebrew worldview, spiritual salvation and physical deliverance complemented one another. There was no rigid dichotomy or mutual exclusion, as many of us operate in today. So when they saw Jesus both preaching and demonstrating the kingdom of God, they expected him to fulfill it physically right away in the limited context of liberating the people of Israel from their oppressors. But Jesus achieved a far greater liberation: the liberation of all humanity and the entire earth from the corruption of death initiated through the broken relationship and resulting sin pandemic.

So what is the unshrunken meaning of the gospel of God's kingdom (Matt. 24:14) or the gospel of Christ (Rom. 15:19)? On one hand, Jesus *is* the gospel, the good news. He is the King who reigns over all kings. Where his kingdom is entered and also expressed, there is wholeness, "peace" in all dimensions: spiritually, psychologically, economically, physiologically.

Secondly, the gospel is the "good news of" something. It cannot be separated from what it stands for. The gospel is the good news of what? Forgiveness of sins and eternal life are the essential foundation, the restoring of the lifeline between humanity and God, our source of life. But here is an ancient key, a secret; salvation is not the whole picture. It is the beginning. The *whole* gospel is the good news of the reign of the good King. The good news is that wherever his kingdom comes into hearts and homes and humanity, it brings the restoration and multiplication of shalom—whole-person, whole-society thriving.

Jesus' Life: Demonstrating God's Kingdom on Earth

During my formative years as a new believer, the spin on the Bible to which I was exposed led me—like many others—into an incomplete picture of the gospel. I thought when Jesus multiplied the fish and bread, this was not about solving world hunger. When he healed sick bodies, it wasn't about making the sick well. When he defended a woman who was about to be stoned, it wasn't about human rights. My religious conditioning led me to believe Jesus' miracles had little or no physical, economic, or social application, the earthly realm serving merely as the vehicle and the stage. I thought the sole purpose was to distinguish him as the Savior of the soul, helping people believe in him and receive eternal life after passing from this world.

This fundamentalist viewpoint is best illustrated by the diagram below on the left. The dark circle represents good activities such as work, education, recreation, and charity. The white circle represents the message of salvation through faith in Christ. When verbal proclamation of the message of soul salvation is viewed as the only "real work of God," then there is little basis for living out and demonstrating God's goodness. Instead of stewarding the earth, instead of creating good things, loving people right where they are, and exemplifying abundant life in the midst of society, we become a segregated subculture attracting well-deserved criticism as being irrelevant anti-social and anti-progress bigots.

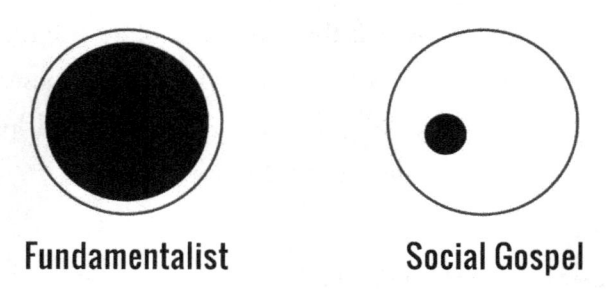

Fundamentalist   **Social Gospel**

The diagram on the right illustrates the opposite extreme. The "social gospel" aims to right the wrongs in the world, but the name and message of Christ is almost fully eclipsed. This extreme can also lead to a performance-based, lifeless religion in which humans, losing sight of Christ's atoning work on the cross, make futile attempts to be good enough for God to accept them.

In both extremes, proclamation of the message of Christ and demonstration of the love of Christ have rigid boundaries and are limited by their exclusion of the other. Both these views represent a manifestation of the partial gospel, a spurious diminution that falls short of the "good news of the kingdom" (Matt. 4:23, Luke 4:43), the "gospel of the kingdom" (Matt. 24:14).

Because we have been unwittingly operating in these errors, the world is not yet reached, multitudes tumble blindly into destruction, and the enemy's pandemics ravage God's good earth and his beloved humans.

The culprit behind both these errors is our deficit in understanding God's nature, his kingdom, and our place in it. For this reason I have taken you through the Scriptures thus far, attempting to offer some of the ancient keys whereby we may, at long last, uncover another secret that the powers of darkness dread you will find. Here it is: A thing that the fundamentalists thought divisive or detrimental to evangelism is the very portal to the most massive turning to Christ in history. Allow me to explain:

> When we allow Christ to be King of all, the gospel is defragmented.

Demonstrational Witnesses

Neither the fundamentalist spiritual-only error nor the social gospel error is novel. Great leaders of the church across the centuries have grappled with the issue of where proclamation and demonstration intersect, and how to integrate the spiritual and the physical in relation to faith.[2]

Is there a priority of one or the other? If we say, "The message, the proclamation of salvation through faith is what really matters," then demonstration falls to the wayside as unimportant, succumbing to dualistic spiritual-secular segregation. If we say, "They are equally important, 'two wings of a plane' " then we lapse into a social gospel.[3] Neglecting to summon people to enter the kingdom through faith in Christ, this trap provides them little besides a more comfortable trip to hell.

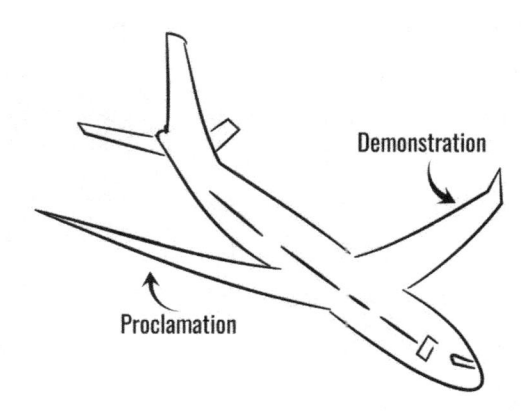

[Illustration of an airplane with arrows labeled "Demonstration" pointing to the wing and "Proclamation" pointing to the nose]

Social gospel error

The answer is revealed by our initial study: God is King and Father, origin and source of all life. Relationship with him means life. Severed relationship means death. Remember the tree whose trunk of "Relationship with God" is cut, whose fruit thenceforth is thorns instead of apples—life that is death-like, corrupted. *All things* enter into death when severed from him. All creation groans (Rom. 8:22). But restored relationship unleashes glorious, redeemed, supernatural *life* because he is the source of life.

Therefore, priority must be given to whatever celebrates and reveals *relationship* with him. But how is this relationship communicated? How is the message delivered? It may not, or at least not initially, be by speaking. The first and essential way in which others must see Christ is by and in our life and actions. I call this being "demonstrational witnesses." If we are living in such a way as to be worthy of representing him, then we have permission to proclaim him by word. Meanwhile, we look for ways to further demonstrate his goodness by action. Thus, the message is carried into hearts on the oil of love.

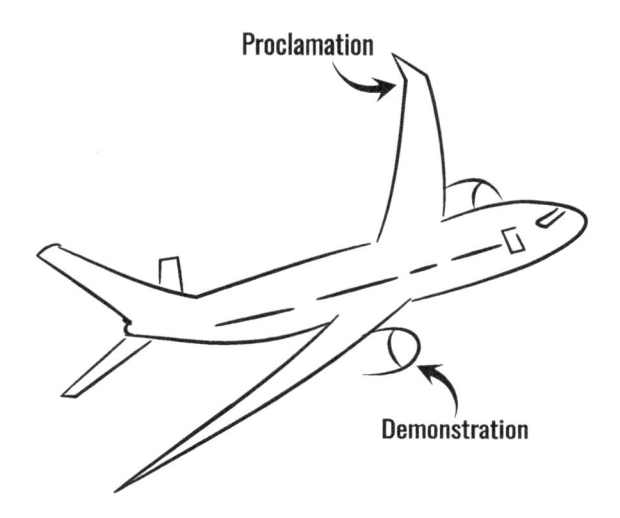

When by the power of the Holy Spirit we are demonstrational witnesses, demonstration is the engine and proclamation, the wings. The two need one another, but they aren't the same. First, the engine must create propulsion. Then the wings can do their job. Love-fueled demonstration must take us to where the people are, to where their felt needs reside—out there in the real world. "By this all people will know that you are my disciples"—not by our doctrine, not even by our words, but by our "love for one another"(John 13:35).

> Demonstration bears witness to the fact that we have something desirable. Then proclamation lifts us and them into heavenly realms, into the presence of the living God who makes them a new creation.

This is why everywhere Jesus went he both proclaimed the good news of the kingdom and also healed every disease and sickness (Matt. 4:23). He both taught the principles of the kingdom and also demonstrated them through defending the oppressed, multiplying food, and opposing injustice.

The outcome of this transformational view and praxis is illustrated in the following simple diagram:

The unashamed message of Jesus' spiritual salvation is central but is carried outward through demonstration, purifying, and transforming whatever it touches. What once was corrupt and dark is enlightened and illumined.

As we rediscover and practice the unified and complete worldview of the Bible, not only will myriads more people become citizens of heaven, but some element of "heaven" will happen throughout every part of life. The unabridged gospel really is good news to the whole world.

Healers and Heralds of Life

What does this mean for us right now? It means the kingdom of life on earth can now "come," as in the Lord's Prayer, to a certain extent. This victory is appropriated first and foremost by individual people putting their faith in Jesus. "Where, O death, is your victory? The sting of death is sin . . . But thanks be to God! He gives us the victory through our Lord Jesus Christ" (1 Cor. 15:55–57).

But remember, Jesus is not only King of heaven; he is King of *all*. His will is that God's "kingdom come" and that God's "will be done" (Matt. 6:10). When? Only in the afterlife? Where? Only in heaven? No! "On earth." What constitutes his will being done? Only the salvation of the soul? To thus limit his goodness is to allow our pagan worldview to hide our inheritance and to shrink God's goodness. It is not the worldview of Jesus, who was a Jew. The Jewish worldview is unifying, not dividing. Jesus had no intention that "on earth as it is in heaven" be limited to what we call salvation, the birthing, our transfer by faith out of the kingdom of darkness and naturalization into the kingdom of God.

> Jesus saw the big picture, those redeemed from spiritual death carrying his life and love into every sector of *now*.

Remember, the creation mandate involved not just maintaining but multiplying, expanding Eden-like beauty and cultivation into the whole earth, making the entire planet a pristine paradise. Therefore Jesus compared what should happen on earth with what is currently happening in the realm of God's spiritual domain, i.e., in "heaven." In that realm is neither death, nor suffering, nor slavery, nor oppression, nor poverty. *This* is what Jesus desires to be manifested also on earth. Like heaven, earth is intended to be "very good." Therefore, Jesus wants to redeem, to heal. Those who so align with his will are "set . . . high above all the nations of the earth. . . . You will be blessed in the city and blessed in the country. The fruit of your womb will be blessed, and the crops of your land" (Deut. 28:1–6). This is not to suggest that everyone who follows Christ is going to become monetarily rich. Neither does "blessed" mean believers are immune from sickness or hardship. Indeed, "all who live godly will suffer persecution" (2 Tim. 3:12). Blessing may come in the form of health, wealth, or influence that we invest back into his kingdom. But it may also come in the form of hardships that provide opportunity for others to see our joy and patience despite our circumstances. Both are a form of blessing.

Formed from earth but imbued with God's Spirit, humans are his authorized representatives on earth. We are commissioned as his deputy-creators and his guardians of good. We are heirs and heralds of eternal life, and also stewards of life on earth. Therefore, those redeemed from death are to be bringers of life in all dimensions. Those victorious through Jesus are now "a royal priesthood, a holy nation"—as Israel was to be—destined to "declare" through word and deed "the praises of him who called you out of darkness into his wonderful light" (1 Pet. 2:9).

So, what is your secret calling? You've collected enough keys now to begin to unlock it: You are dangerous to the powers of darkness! You are dangerous to poverty, oppression, and every earthly pandemic. You are far more powerful than you thought. And here is your awesome, royal commission:

> Wherever a manifestation of death is active, you are called to permeate it with life.

When Jesus said, "You are the light of the world" and "You are the salt of the earth," he actually meant it (Matt. 5:13–14)! We are to heal what is diseased, preserve what is good, season what is bland, guide what is lost, and reveal what is true. He did not intend us to spiritualize it down to something less than that which is fitting for the Father, Creator, and King of all things. We are authorized and equipped by his Spirit to release life in the place of death, love instead of hate or neglect, and liberty where there is injustice or oppression. We are to imbue flavor, prevent decay, and shine hope into a diseased and groaning world.

Now, let's see how King Jesus worked through Mike, Renae, and others to see his kingdom come to a suicide- and drug- ridden town.

6

CASE STUDY - SUICIDE TO SHALOM

*"If my people, who are called by my name,
will humble themselves and pray and seek my face and
turn from their wicked ways, then I will hear from heaven,
and I will forgive their sin and will heal their land."*

—2 Chron. 7:14

*"Left to ourselves we lapse into a kind of collusion with entropy,
acquiescing in the general belief that things may be getting
worse but that there's nothing much we can do about them.
And we are wrong. Our task in the present...
is to live as resurrection people in between
Easter and the final day."*

—N. T. Wright

1880: *The Sin and the Curse*

The pinto's iron-tough hooves picked their way around cacti and boulders, pressing on toward the summit. His rider, honored for decades as an expert hunter and warrior, did not sit tall as he once did. He rode hunched over, looking neither ahead nor to the side. There was nothing to see. Nothing more to hope for. Eyes glassy and defeated, his expressionless stare fell upon the terrain from which his people were, as of this day, officially banished.

The trail was barely visible, trodden by few, for it was a dead end, offering sudden death to the unwary traveler. Sensing danger, the pony hesitated. His rider urged him on a few more yards, then slid off. The reins dropped on the ground signaled break time for the pony. He went about seeking edible shrubs that eked out an existence, drawing moisture from nighttime dews.

Copper-brown moccasin-clad feet trudged onward a few more yards. There at the summit, the earth ceased to exist. The trail ended in a sheer two-thousand-foot drop. Below lay the junction of the Colorado and Gunnison, silver-blue, serpentining across the fertile plain, capable of supporting life of every kind—crops, wildlife, and herds. Beyond the river to the east rose majestic Grand Mesa, black-green with lush conifers.

The old chief's weather- and hardship-leathered face defied the emotions that seethed in his heart. His eyes, cold with sorrow and pain, narrowed as he gazed across the green and gold-brown paradise below, hazy blue in the distance where it met the sky. This beautiful land of snow-crowned peaks and streaming rivers, spawning trout, and rutting elk belonged to his people, the Ute. Their name meant "people of the mountains." But the settlers had stolen the mountains. Treaty after treaty had been enacted, only to be broken as greed overcame any sense of morality and justice. Now settlements of westward migrants dotted the plain below.

Far away on the horizon a forlorn troupe traveled westward. Most walked, some rode ponies. Like their chief, their eyes were fixed on the earth. Defeated and demoralized, they were the last to be driven from this northwestern Colorado region. Herded by military officers, they trudged away from their homeland, banished to a reservation on a piece of desert where for generations they would languish in hopelessness and dependency on government handouts.

Rage flared the chief's nostrils. He could sense that Great Spirit shared his pain, his anger. The time had come. The time for vengeance. "Our muskets are too few," he murmured. "We are outnumbered. We cannot fight with guns. So now we must do what we can to avenge our people."

There were no trees on the plateau, but the plenteous supply of dry shrubs would suffice. His hands gathered them into a heap. Then from a pouch he withdrew a match. One strike on flint and the bonfire roared. Then he waited, scanning the pinnacle of Grand Mesa and the painted cliffs in the far distance to the west. In a few moments, a fire blazed on the Mesa. And soon after, though too distant to see the blaze, smoke rose on the western cliffs. He and his fellow Ute leaders had converged on these three high places for one united purpose: to avenge the capture of their ancestral territory.

Ceremoniously, the chief bent down and in each hand scooped up a fistful of earth. Looking through the flames, he gazed out across the valley. Then rising to his full height, Chief Colorow extended his buckskin-clad arms toward the fire and began letting the dust fall into it. The setting sun stretched his shadow long across the rocky ground. A single eagle's pinion braided into his jet-black hair—a defiant statement of his heritage—quivered in the bonfire's rising heat. Past the flames he stared down upon the homesteads with their fences and cattle, their oxen and mules and wagons, their women in flowing dresses and children cavorting about. As the crackling sagebrush sent smoke plumes into the sky, and as the earth continued to fall from his hands, he filled his lungs and opened his lips. In the language of his people he cried out to whatever spirits or powers would give ear to his pain.

"This land belongs to the Ute!" His voice echoed across the valley, but so lofty was the precipice upon which he stood, it would not carry to human ears. That was of little importance. His intent was to speak to spiritual ears. The chief repeated, with more vehemence, "This land belongs to the Ute! The settlers have stolen it from us. They wanted it for themselves. Now they have it. They have their wishes. By lies and plagues, by bloodshed and dishonesty, they have severed us from our land." He paused, drawing great deep breaths, filling his lungs with the pristine air. "Therefore, I now pronounce a curse upon this valley. White man . . ."

A sudden burst of wind picked up dust, twisting it into a whirlwind. In the sky above, cloudless turquoise earlier, dark clouds had begun to boil. With renewed fervor, throwing into the proclamation the last of his fighting spirit, the chief screamed into the rising storm, "WHITE MAN, YOU WILL DIE HERE!"

☙ ⋅⋅ ❧

The same year, Pennsylvania-born businessman George A. Crawford heard that the former Ute lands were now open for settlement. He traveled there and by September had surveyed and initiated plans for a city to be built at the confluence of the Colorado and Gunnison Rivers. With the founding of Grand Junction, the Grand Valley region developed rapidly as settlers arrived in droves.

2011: Eight Ball Street.

Appropriately named Clifton, the spectacular Book Cliffs and skyward-jutting Mount Garfield overshadowed the little suburb of Grand Junction. We introduced Pastors Mike and Rennae in chapter 4. They rented a house on 32 One-Eighth Road and started New Day Church in the same area. The locals call that street "32 and an Eight Ball," referencing an eighth of an ounce of cocaine. The Lord had brought them to the red-light district of drug addiction!

In the beginning, they weren't ready for what God wanted to do. "Alignment had to happen, changing our hearts so we could carry transformation," said Mike. "Until you're transformed, you're not going to be a transformer."

Rennae says, "We were praying for the compassion Jesus had when he came to the edge of the city and wept over it. We were seeking God, being broken over our broken community."

Repentance in Place of Curses

Many years earlier, Mike had hiked up to the top of Mount Garfield. There he saw a vision of fires burning on the three high places surrounding the valley: Mount Garfield, Grand Mesa, and the National Monument. The fires were ceremonial blazes lit for a specific purpose. Standing behind the fires were Native Americans. Demoralized and angry, robbed of their land, their hearts were bitter as they pronounced a curse over the valley, inviting the spirit of death. The Lord was allowing Mike to see into the past, to see what had occurred. Death had been pronounced over the valley.

The first action steps to which the Lord led Mike, Rennae, and other team members was to ask forgiveness for the sins of the early settlers. By doing so, they began the work of closing spiritual doorways by which the demonic powers of death had access to the land.

Mike and Rennae were not the only ones in whose hearts the Lord was birthing the healing vision. Others who became key participants in what would follow included Amy Everett, director of Colorado Prays and regional prayer leader for Transform Our World (TOW), Pastor Jim Hale, leader of the Grand Junction Ministerial Alliance, Tim Tyler, director of Colorado Coalition for Apostolic Transformation (CCAT), and many Native American churches. Mike himself was part Native American, and together with the Native leaders, they prayed, worshipped, and repented on behalf of the land.

The kingdom of life was battering the gates and government of darkness. But the battle had only just begun. The kingdom of darkness, which had been granted access through a previous generation's sin, would fight back all the harder.

August 2018: The Stockade.

Suicide had always plagued Mesa County, but it reached a five-year high in 2018, with nearly four times more lives lost than the national average.[1] Among the drug overdoses and self-inflicted shootings, fourteen were teenagers. That year Mesa had the highest number of suicides per capita in Colorado, and the state was ranked sixth worst in the nation.

The epidemic of death catalyzed action. But it wasn't a conference or bringing in a famous speaker that started the movement. A simple email sent by an unnamed believer declared, "Enough is enough! Join me at the school flagpole. We're going to *pray*!" The email went viral. Believers all over the valley gathered at school flagpoles to pray. Soon churches across the county were rallying together in prayer for healing and hope and an end to the pandemic of death.

I had known Mike and Rennae for many years. They exuded the presence of Christ, and whenever they prayed and declared the will and word of God, I could sense the realms of darkness being shaken. The rare times that my ministry travels allowed downtime at my mom's house on the Western Slope, I often saw them at other meetings farther south. But my scant contact with Grand Junction or Clifton consisted of enjoying the incredible view of Mount Garfield while whizzing through on my way back and forth to Denver. I had never studied the history of the valley.

Therefore, when Mike invited me to minister for New Day Church in August 2018, I was unaware of the spiritual or historic brokenness of the region, or of the death that was running rampant in the city at that very moment.

After an inspiring time of ministry with their congregation, it was time to pray and declare God's will over the city. That is when the exciting things started to happen! The Lord showed me a vision. I saw Mount Garfield and the entire city surrounded by a high and ancient fence built of upright posts set into the ground—a stockade. It was an Old West version of a Jericho wall, and it encircled the valley and the mountain.

Then the stockade fell down flat, and God's glory began to shine out across the valley, turning everything bright and filling it with life. Then I heard, "Death has lost its sting!"

At the same time, Mike was getting a similar vision. We began to pray and to declare life and healing over the valley. Then I knew the next step that must be taken—to physically go to the high places and invite God's healing and restoration over the valley. I asked Mike, "Has anyone ever gone up on Mt Garfield and blown a shofar and invited God's presence and wholeness?"

He replied, "Not that I know of."

That set in motion a plan that I believe the Lord had reserved for the right timing.

2019: Storming the Gates of Death

Mike and Rennae's team, joined by Amy and others, mobilized the Lord's hosts for a grand storming of the gates of death.

This initiative occurred on March 16, 2019. Armed with shofars, three "gorilla teams" of seasoned intercessors set out, one bound for Grand Mesa, another for the National Monument, and Mike and Jim's team hiked the two thousand feet up to the top of Mount Garfield. At the three high points where the Holy Spirit had shown Mike the curses being released, the intercessors praised and extolled Jesus by whose blood we are redeemed from the curse (Gal. 3:13). In a coordinated assault on the government of darkness, they attacked the spirit of death, commanding it to come down in the name of Jesus. At 10:00 a.m. those bearing the instrument that symbolizes the voice of the King of all lifted shofars toward heaven. With one voice the shofars sounded and the intercessors shouted victory, declaring life and peace over the Grand Valley.

Simultaneously the Lord showed Mike another vision. He saw the Colorado and Gunnison Rivers begin to rise. They rose and rose until they filled the valley, all the way up to the mountain peaks. The river of God's cleansing and healing presence was rising! Mike had never before felt the power and authority of the Holy Spirit as he did in that moment.

Throughout the remainder of the day, 225 believers from a wide array of churches—including Native Americans, whites, blacks, and Hispanics—assembled in a church parking lot. After the leaders formed them into seventy-five teams, each team was assigned two or three locations for prayer, 170 locations in all. The teams were coached to focus on Jesus, not the devil. They were not to spend time shouting at the false prince of death, but to praise and exalt the true King of life. Neither would they focus on entities traditionally viewed as "strongholds" of darkness. Instead, piling into seventy-five cars, the intercessors went to every government building, every church facility, and every school in the city. Their assignment was to invite God's will to be done and his blessing to come to that institution or location and to the people associated with it.

The three gorilla teams also went to spiritual stronghold locations to continue closing the doorways of sin and breaking curses over the city. That night a grand worship blowout was held at the Vineyard Church. The worship leaders were Native Americans, praising the Lord and declaring the victory of Jesus' resurrection, celebrating his healing in the land.

Ute Courthouse and Police Blessing

Prayer and worship are essential and foundational building blocks, but they aren't the whole story. A foundation had been laid. Now there was more work to do.

In the months that followed, the Ute tribal leaders invited Mike and his team to come and dedicate their new courthouse. This was a groundbreaking first, indicating that true reconciliation had occurred all the way to the government level.

Police officers began to reach out to the community, knocking on doors and introducing themselves. In the past, when a police officer spotted a drug dealer, they drove on by. But now they stopped, got out of the car, and talked to him. This simple relational outreach made a huge impact in the community . . . and it also influenced the church. The officers started to say to church leaders, "We're getting out of our cars to connect with people. Now you need to get out of your buildings and do the same!"

Meanwhile, the ongoing prayer meetings were transformed when they began to invite city leaders to come and speak to them. The first guest Jim invited was the city commissioner. Representatives from ten to fifteen churches learned about the challenges and needs of the government sector; then they gathered around the commissioner and his team and prayed for them and blessed them.

"Always before, you Christians just cared about your religious agenda," commented the commissioner. "But now I see that you care about the people and the city. Thank you. Now I see that your God really is love."

Next, the Christian leaders reached out to business leaders. Most of these were Christians. After the businessmen had spoken, Jim went forward and got down on his knees. He asked forgiveness, confessing that in the past, he had wanted businesspeople to become members of his church in hopes that they would give large offerings. Other pastors joined him in repentance. The business leaders had tears in their eyes. Right after that assembly, six or seven of those leaders started prayer meetings in their places of business. Others realized they were called to be an example of excellence and improved their treatment of employees.

These united learning/prayer gatherings continued; special invitees included representatives of media, law enforcement, the military, government, judges, first responders, marketplace leaders, educators ,and others. At every event something powerful and awesome happened, and the participants felt a further shift.

2019 and Beyond: Shalom Comes to Clifton

The healing that had been released across the city by prayer, reconciliation, the collaboration of churches, and the engagement and honoring of civic and community leaders all began to bear tangible fruit:

Drug related deaths dropped by 50 percent.

In Clifton, burglary and car theft declined by 41 percent.

Child abuse was reduced by 33 percent.

Sex crimes declined by 50 percent.

And whereas the year before fourteen teens had committed suicide, in 2019 there was only one teen suicide.

Development began to come to the city. Many organizations invested money to improve Clifton. It was just one more sign that God's river had risen, the stockade—the spirit of death—had fallen, and the King of all was healing the land through the prayer and active engagement of people who were operating in their secret calling.

In the following years Jim carried the movement further by dressing up as Captain Kindness and bringing the biblical value of honor for one another to schools throughout the city. He testified, "The atmosphere in the city is totally changed. The darkness is gone. Now there is hope, peace, and life."

Mike says, "What we're seeing is the manifestation of the level at which we've engaged God. If we want to see more, engage him at a deeper level. Transformation comes when the presence of God touches something." All real healing comes forth from Jesus, the Healer.

What are the bulwarks of the enemy in your town? Maybe you are called to be the woman at the flagpole or the couple who initiates reconciliation. Maybe you're called to befriend someone who is very much *un*like you, outside your comfortable *oikos*, and thereby catalyze healing. Remember, you are *imago dei*, a royal ambassador of heaven to earth. Where can you bring the Father's love into relationships?

Where can you bring the Creator's innovation into science? Where can you bring the good King's leadership into management or stewardship? Royal ambassador, you have a higher purpose than the principalities of darkness would like you to believe.

7

THE MYSTERY CHURCH

"His intent was that now, through the church, the manifold wisdom of God should be made known to the rulers and authorities in the heavenly realms."

—Eph. 3:10

"[The early church was] a thermostat that transformed the mores of society. [It operated under] the conviction that they were a "colony of heaven" . . . Small in number, they were big in commitment . . . By their effort and example they brought an end to such ancient evils as infanticide and gladiatorial contests."

—Martin Luther King Jr.

Cost of Partial Identity

The spiritual powers of darkness dread the possibility that Jesus' individual citizens might apprehend their secret calling. But they quake with multiplied terror at the thought that the organized church might discover God's highest purpose: that Jesus promised to build not a mere religion, not a mere service that takes place in a special building, not even a community that gathers primarily for fellowship, worship, and learning. When "church" becomes what Jesus envisioned, a joyous wind of healing and wholeness, freedom, and peace will be released across every sector of life. The works of darkness—evil in all its forms, in every life and every community—will be dealt a blow in the same way that penicillin shrivels harmful bacteria.

So dangerous to the devil's agenda was Christ's vision for His church that from the beginning, the kingdom of death leveraged all its resources to both contain and corrupt it. The kingdom of darkness succeeded and continues to succeed in its agenda due to our incomplete understanding of God, creation, Christ, and ourselves. Throughout history up to the present day, believers in general operate on the defensive, containing our light under a basket. Others corrupt themselves by doing evil, thus nullifying their authority. Almost all of us unknowingly fragment the gospel because our worldview contains some degree of dualism.

Because of these errors, in our modern world "Christianity has come to represent hypocrisy, judgmentalism, anti-intellectualism, insensitivity, and bigotry,"[1] the church being regarded as "irrelevant and immoral."[2] In some nations Christians are stigmatized as traitorous vestiges of colonialism, culture cancellers, and propagators of a foreign religion.

But as we'll see in just a few more paragraphs, the true church—those who love and reflect Christ as genuine disciples—has brought more good into the world than any other group, culture, nation, or community in history. How can a movement that did so much good across the centuries be today considered undesirable, outdated, or irrelevant? Because our calling has been secret! Because long ago we lost the ancient keys! Therefore we languish under a diminished understanding of ourselves as believers and of churches in particular.

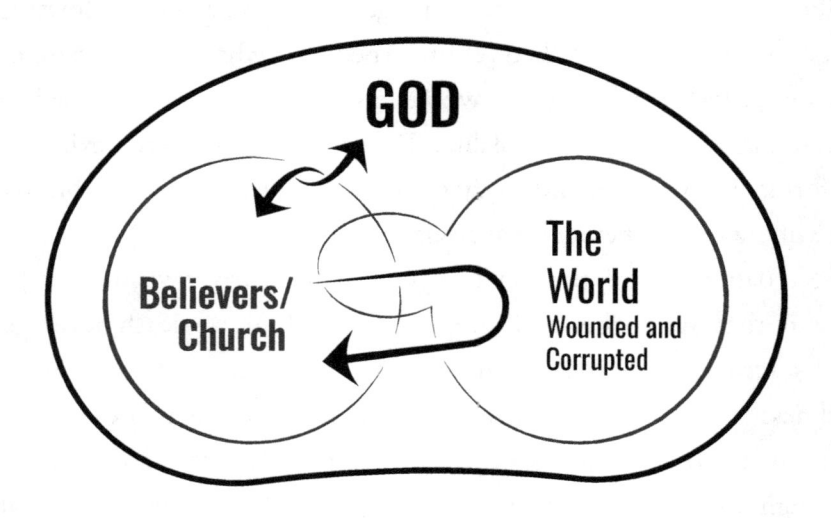

```
         GOD
    ↙↗
 ┌─────────────────────────────┐
 │   ┌─────────┐   ┌─────────┐ │
 │   │Believers/│   │  The    │ │
 │   │ Church  │   │ World   │ │
 │   │         │   │Wounded and│
 │   │         │   │Corrupted │ │
 │   └─────────┘   └─────────┘ │
 └─────────────────────────────┘
```

This diagram depicts today's average believer and church community. God encompasses all, because he is King of all. But he has delegated the stewardship of Earth to humans. "The world" refers to people separated from a relationship with their Father God, and human systems victimized by the sin pandemic—dishonesty in business, oppression in government, abuse in marriage, etc.—thus reflecting the rule of the enemy's kingdom. The U-shaped arrow indicates that believers—the church—are leading some individuals to salvation. But there's a problem:

> Our partial paradigm extracts souls and ejects them to heaven. The biblical paradigm makes disciples and injects them into the world to multiply and heal.

Consciously or not, we have often operated as "segregated from" the world while making "bombing raids" to extract souls. Dallas Willard terms this dysfunction "the great omission."[3] In this extraction model, the rule of evil in the world remains unchallenged, and believers are often viewed as irrelevant vestiges of outdated superstitions. The masses are left with the calamitous perception that Christian faith is just one more religion, or a killjoy, or even a social parasite.

Meanwhile the stuff pushing into the church illustrates that the church itself is being "discipled" by the evil, infiltrated by elements of the kingdom of darkness. Believers operate on the defensive and succumb to the sin pandemic, failing to exemplify core characteristics of Christ's kingdom such as purity, self-control, and forgiveness.

A survey of Christians ages eighteen to twenty-nine found that they want to be genuine disciples of Christ but without segregating themselves from the people, culture and activities around them. They want to follow Jesus while still connecting with the world they live in, rather than segregating from it. However, because this desire is rarely affirmed by the organized church, they also believe that God is more at work outside the church than inside.[4][5] The Lord is using these youngsters to show the rest of us the way, but are we listening? Our persistent partial identity has left believers uncertain about whether or how we are to influence life on earth. Of course we are to purify our lives from sinful thoughts and deeds. Of course we are to be witnesses by sharing Christ with others. But our dualism, our sacred-secular divide, has confused us as to whether we really have any further mandate. The awesome news is, there's *so much more*!

So far you've received the essential keys to escape from the partial identity, the shrunken gospel, into the liberty of the gospel of God's kingdom. But you've not yet arrived. Your calling is still somewhat secret. Another layer of God's highest purpose lies concealed. This pivotal ancient key is contained in the *name* that our Deliverer King bestowed upon his kingdom community—ekklesia.

Ekklesia

For three years Jesus modeled a life of power and love, holiness without legalism, quietly revolutionary and peacefully transformational. He announced and demonstrated the kingdom, the dawning of the reign of God, the good Father King. Then Jesus inaugurated his community. Over those who had put their faith in him, following him as true disciples, he declared a name. Encapsulated in that name lay a path never trodden by human beings.

"On this rock I will build My church [ekklesia], and the gates of Hades shall not prevail against it" (Matt. 16:18 NKJV). The word *ekklesia* appears 115 times in the New Testament. In the 112 times that it refers to Christians or their assemblies, our English translations render it "church." Perhaps you have heard the word *ekklesia* before. That which in our time may sound foreign and mysterious was not so in the time of Jesus. Ekklesia was to every Roman and Jew what *congress, senate,* or *parliament* is to people today.

Ekklesia (ekk-le-see'-ah) is a simple compound of the Greek words *ek* ("out of") and *kaleo* ("called"). Hence, it is often defined as "the called-out ones." In the old covenant God's people were first called to leave Ur (Gen. 12:1), then Egypt (Exod. 12:17), and finally Babylon (Isa. 48:20; Ezek. 36:24). Believers are called out of spiritual darkness, called out of death to inherit eternal life through Jesus Christ. We are called out of sin to be "separated unto" God, purifying our hearts and our actions, living lives of moral purity (Isa. 52:11; 2 Cor. 6:17).

This is all well and good. But the word *ekklesia* enjoys a rich and ancient history, and "called-out ones" falls short of its full definition. To dissect it and only look at its parts is like choking down a cup of flour, a cup of sugar, two raw eggs, and a spoonful of leavening without considering that, if mixed together and baked, the resulting pastry would bring sheer delight!

Likewise, most of what we call "church" today falls short of Jesus' vision. Before we encounter what Jesus intended to found, we must understand what the early community of God's kingdom was like and where we drifted astray.

What Jesus Founded: A Movement That Brought Healing

Jesus did not found a religion but a movement. This movement restored citizenship in God's kingdom and eternal life to those who believed, and infused healing and hope into all of life. Christianity was never intended to be perceived as one of the world religions, but as Jesus is "the way, the truth and the life" (John 14:6) so also what he founded would be the doorway by which human life might thrive. This is clear when we observe that Jesus discipled both Jewish pre-Christians and a polytheistic Gentile society by being radically contrary to religious legalism and radically relevant to the earth.

When he healed sick bodies, delivered people from demonic torment, and raised Lazarus from the dead, he demonstrated God's healing life triumphing over the devil's pandemic of sickness and death.

When he fed the multitudes, he demonstrated God's will of economic abundance in the face of the devil's pandemic of poverty.

> Jesus invaded corrupt human systems and the devil's reign of death, not with finite human revolution, nor with religious rules, but with God's righteous and merciful reign.

When he pardoned the woman who was about to be stoned, he demonstrated God's kingdom principle of mercy and equality of the sexes against the devil's pandemic of violence and sexism.

When he declared the parable of the good Samaritan, he pronounced God's kingdom principle of racial equal rights and equal value in the face of the devil's pandemic of racism. He ministered alike to rich and poor, black and white, Jew and Gentile, infirm and robust, citizen and alien, prince and pauper.

He could be found both physically and emotionally wherever human beings were—marketplace and streets, bazaar, and banquet, well and wedding, holy places and unholy places, from red light districts to the homes of robbers, religious leaders and revolutionaries.

> Jesus operated above society's sinful ways while yet dynamically engaging with society itself.

He was sinless while loving sinners in the trenches. Thus, he ignited not a mere religion, not only the way to soul salvation, but a nation-discipling, world-transforming peaceful revolution. He called whole communities into the beauteous vision of "on earth as it is in heaven" (Matt. 6:10).

The early Kingdom citizens took his healing balm to the ends of the earth. Through them the Holy Spirit did the same miracles he had done through Christ, healing sick bodies and delivering those tormented by demons. They then invited people into citizenship through repentance and faith in the risen King Jesus. To serve their patients they frequented both Jewish synagogues and pagan agoras. The streets and marketplaces were their pulpit and their practice.

The movement did not expand through violence as would Islam a few centuries later. It did not endorse coercion, bribery, or force, but grew by proclaiming Jesus' message and by demonstrating his living power to heal souls, bodies, and humanity as a whole. The Greek word for "witness" is *martus*. As unashamed witnesses to "another King, one called Jesus," the movement was viewed as dangerous and subversive (Acts 17:7). Because they refused to do obeisance to idols or emperors, Christians were deemed "vain and insane," "reprobate characters" promoting a "new and malevolent superstition."[6]

Meanwhile though, the Christian community achieved a "sociological impossibility:"[7] Despite the prevailing culture which practiced extreme segregation, racism, and discrimination, in the kingdom community Jew and Roman, male and female, slave and free all became one family. Racism was terminated, baffling the entire surrounding world. Tertullian, one of the first Christian leaders after the original Apostles and Paul, wrote of how Christians were perceived: "'Only look,' they say, 'look how they love one another!' (they themselves being given to mutual hatred). 'Look how they are prepared to die for one another!' (they themselves being readier to kill each other)."[8] So different were the Christians from anything the world had seen that they were by 200 AD referred to as a "third race,"[9] exemplifying impeccable moral character.

Their influence wasn't limited to preaching or personal piety, nor was it restricted to their own tribe. As unashamed witnesses of a disruptive higher way, the Christians came to be known as demonstrators of the "gospel of love and charity."[10] A new language had dawned upon the world, "the language of love. But it was more than a language, it was a thing of power and action."[11] They embodied a whole new lifestyle—loving unconditionally, forgiving their persecutors, treating women with respect and servants with justice.

Following the example of Jesus their founder, they carried forward his heritage, offering charity to the forsaken and equal rights for the oppressed. They served, defended, and elevated those whom the prevailing culture of that era despised: the poor, the orphaned, the sick, the elderly, and the unborn. "It is our care for the helpless, our practice of loving kindness," wrote Tertullian, "that brands us in the eyes of many of our opponents."[12] Such was their love and service to the oppressed that they were declared to be "the ones who hold the world together."[13]

This life-giving, soul-saving, and nation-transforming movement carried the grand message of God's kingdom reign, his healing love and salvation, his deliverance from the death pandemic to the entire known world through both word and deed.

These early disciples were living out their secret calling. They were fulfilling God's highest purpose. By the fourth century, kingdom citizens had made disciples and established communities of faith throughout nearly the entire Roman Empire. They had also elevated the value of human life, promoted marriage and family, and founded the world's first modern hospitals.[14] All these things were revolutionary in Greco-Roman society.[15] "The Way," as the kingdom community was initially known, was just that—it showed and provided the way by which human beings were intended to live, from their personal lives to their communities, cities, and nations (Acts 9:2). It embodied his kingdom "on earth as in heaven."

Thus, in its fledgling stage the community came very close to what Jesus had intended – it was, truly, his ekklesia.

But after a short time, a tragic drift ensued. "The early church reduced its understanding of its own calling and allowed itself to become one more religion."[16] Even the earliest church fathers embraced a creeping gnostic dualism, along with the infiltration of legalism and works-based justification. The awareness of Jesus as healer King and of his community as the ekklesia, the legislative body of his kingdom on earth, began to wane. Like political parties, Christians drifted either "left" or "right." On the right, "People's expectations came to be focused on heaven rather than on this world and God's involvement in history; instead of looking forward to the future they looked up to eternity."[17]

Those who veered off to the "left," lost the foundation of salvation by faith and allowed social activism to take the place of the cross. The kingdom of God was reduced to "a gospel of sin management"[18] at one extreme and humanism at the other. Both extremes fell short of the ideal presented by Jesus, and the movement deviated into a partial revelation, an incomplete gospel.

That the Scriptures employ the word *ekklesia* for Christ's community has monumental connotations. Tragically, the powerful meaning of this word has been kept secret for centuries. It holds an ancient key to unleash our secret calling.

Citizens of a Spiritual Nation

When God assembled the people of Israel and made his covenant with them, it was called "the day of the *qahal* [assembly]." (Deut. 9:10) It constituted the legislative convening of a spiritual nation, God's kingdom representatives on earth.

In the time of Christ, the Greek version of the Old Testament, called the Septuagint, was popular. Therein *ekklesia* was the most common word used to translate the Hebrew *qahal*. The legislative nature of the Old Testament assembly is affirmed by the choice of the word *ekklesia*.[19] When the New Testament Scriptures carry the use of ekklesia over to the church, it confirms that like old covenant Israel, Jesus' new covenant disciples were to be seen not as adherents to one among many religions, but as citizens of a spiritual nation. They constituted his "holy nation" (1 Pet. 2:9), his kingdom and priests (Rev. 1:6; 5:10).

Old Covenant Israel was also to be a community that reflected God's kingdom on earth—entered by faith but then lived out actively and publicly among all nations, cultures, and societies (Isa. 42:6). As Israel assembled to worship God and receive His Law, likewise the new covenant ekklesia assembles to receive God's word and power, then is sent forth as his witnesses, demonstrating and proclaiming his good and redeeming reign (Phil. 2:15–16).

But because Jesus is King, he also intended his citizens and assembly to include certain characteristics of the Greco-Roman ekklesia.

Legislators Promoting Life Where There Is Death

In the time of Christ, ekklesia was an important part of Roman government, the assembling together of citizens to steward and guide their community. The Greek lexicon defines *ekklesia* as "a gathering of citizens called-out from their homes into some public place," "an assembly of the people . . . for the purpose of deliberating."[20] Thus, when Jesus said, "I will build my ekklesia," the disciples would have naturally understood Jesus' intent; his community was called out to assemble for a distinct reason. But they didn't think, "Oh, we're being called out of sin." That had already happened by their allegiance to Christ! They had already been grafted into the good vine, naturalized into his kingdom as citizens. So what was next? *Ekklesia*! An assembly of Jesus' New Covenant kingdom citizens, with the mission of incarnating and disseminating his righteous stewardship and healing in the earth!

> The church was to be the Deliverer King's legislative body "called out" in order to be "sent into" the world as his ambassadors.

According to the context of Matthew 16, Jesus will build a dynamic, outwardly engaged, powerfully wise, kindness-demonstrating, love-embodying, healing-imparting citizenship that will transform from the inside out both individuals and cultures. After all, Jesus is both Priest and King, so what Jesus would build was to be both priestly and kingly. As high priest he would reconcile humans back to God, healing the sin pandemic at the core. As King, Jesus would carry that foundational healing forth into healing of life as a whole—a healing that will be fulfilled in its entirety only when he returns, when "the kingdoms of this world" shall become "the kingdoms of our Lord" (Rev. 11:15 NKJV).

Religion is too small for the king who owns it all. God made humans body, mind, and spirit and called it "very good." Jesus healed people's bodies, and he himself rose bodily from the grave. Likewise, Jesus' ekklesia will influence not exclusively spirit but also body and mind, unleashing shalom.

What should today's assembly of the kingdom look like? Everything we consider core to a church service—teaching and study of Scripture, singing and musical worship, prayer, fellowship, giving, baptism, and celebrating Communion—are all good. Every citizen of Christ's kingdom should be a committed participant in a community of believers (Heb. 10:25). The "local church" is essential to the kingdom presence in any community.

But here is the key: the ekklesia assembly is not limited to an official "service" in which all or most of the above are carried out on a weekly basis. Neither do those activities form the end goal of the assembly envisioned by Jesus. The overarching purpose is contained and communicated in the context and rich history of the word *ekklesia*.

"The concept of *qahal* and its Greek counterpart *ekklesia* describe a redeemed people who are summoned and assembled to learn and apply God's life-giving law to their own lives, then to accomplish the business of heaven on the earth. The called-out of Moses and the called-out of Christ were duly summoned representatives,

> The church that Jesus will build is destined to legislate our Father-King's salvation and wholeness into every corner of creation.

disciples with a purpose, agencies of kingdom government, a ruling council or legislative body."[21] Salvation is the essential rite of admission, followed by character formation. Membership in Christ's ekklesia thenceforth is to be outward focused, incarnating and fulfilling an office of responsibility, legislating the will and principles of the King into his world.

The Glorious Purpose of Christ's Ekklesia

Membership in Christ's ekklesia means entering a twofold adventure: First, believers are to be healers through bearing witness to the risen king Jesus, who triumphed over the pandemic of sin and death. Whoever believes in the completed work of Jesus on the cross is cleansed of the leprosy of sin, healed of the separation it caused, grafted into the good vine, adopted into God's family, naturalized as citizens of his kingdom (Eph. 2:19; Phil. 3:20). We become a "new creation. Old things have passed away" (2 Cor. 5:17 NKJV). Through proclamation and demonstration we then take this spiritual reconciliation and redemption to "Jerusalam (family or city), Judea (local community or nation), Samaria (the marginalized or despised), and the ends of the earth (distant lands, especially those who have no access to the gospel) (Acts 1:8; Mark 16). Christ's blood is applied, and what was dead springs to life; what was diseased is healed. The pandemic is zapped at its root. The kingdom of life is populated, and the kingdom of death is plundered. This is the core of the Great Commission.

Arising out of this soil like a plant from good ground, like a building upon a strong foundation, is the second aspect of reconciliation. We are to serve as his healers of life here and now. "The Son of Man has come to seek and to save that which was lost" (Luke 19:10 NASB). All that was "lost" in the fall is to be restored. All that relates to life on earth—relationship, creativity, and guardianship—is to be brought into "at-one-ment" with life's good Author and King. He desires to restore what was lost by healing our souls, bodies, minds, and all creation. As the image of the Creator, imago dei, we are authorized and deputized to create and invent new things, taking what God made and stewarding, cultivating it into forms of usefulness and beauty, expression and resourcefulness, industry, and freedom. As his ekklesia we are, by his Spirit, to be leaders guiding the world into the Healer's life-giving ways, privileged to represent the King as examples across all sectors of culture. That physical restoration is realized partially now and fully when Christ returns.

How can the partial gospel be completed? How can the omission be remedied? How can Christ's church enter her secret calling as his powerful, love-motivated, pure-living, grace-broadcasting, wound-healing ekklesia?

Compare the previous diagram to the one below. In this second diagram is depicted the ekklesia that Christ desires to build—the church operating in its full identity, dynamically engaged, influencing without being corrupted, sent into the midst of the world to incarnate and actuate his kingdom of life in the midst of its swirling troubles and tribulations.

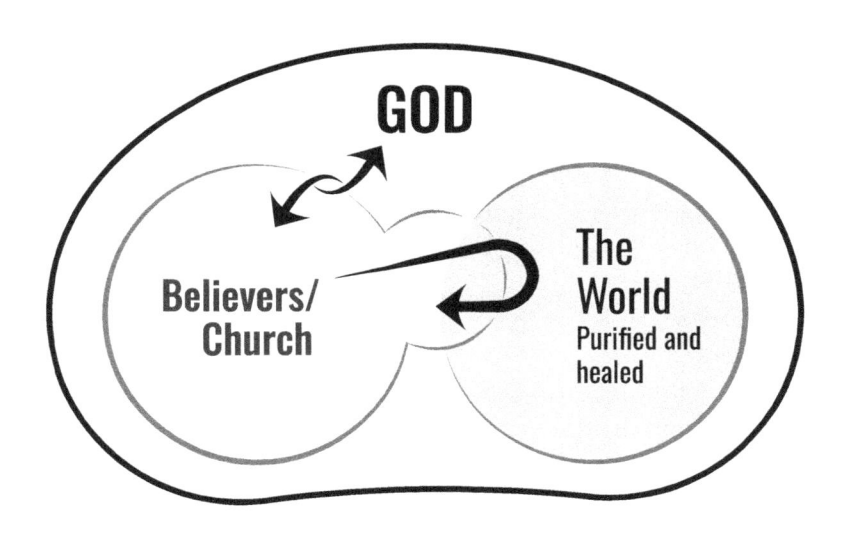

The thicker U-shaped line indicates that far more people are coming to salvation. This is because we aren't merely extracting souls, but making disciples who take God's goodness *into* the world. But they don't stop with the message of soul salvation. Illustrated by the white area pushing into the dark, these discipled believers are redeeming life's activities. They demonstrate and promote characteristics of heaven such as honesty in business, good governance, and family values.

Now the church is no longer being infiltrated, but rather is influencing the world around it. The rule of evil is mitigated, and the masses see God's kingdom expressed through believers intentionally living as his image bearers in the world. The ekklesia may be embraced as an "essential service" in the community, or it may be opposed, but it will no longer be irrelevant or ignored!

What is the business of Christ's kingdom? What is the business of his ekklesia? It is not gazing into heaven waiting for Jesus to return. It is not bickering over doctrinal trivia (Titus 3:9; 1 Tim. 1:4). And let us desist from looking at the evil in the world and whining that we are powerless to change it and abdicated from the responsibility to do so. As darkness is the absence of light, evil is the absence of good. It must flee when we arise! Through the Holy Spirit who dwells in us we are therefore both powerful and responsible!

> The Great Physician's finished work on the cross authorized and initiated the legal healing of the pandemic of sin with all its expressions. Now our privilege is to allow that healing to flow through us into all sectors of life—the earthly here and the eternal hereafter.

Now you have a framework for a bigger influence! When you enter your secret calling as a healer of earth's pandemic, incredible things can happen. Like this . . .

Mini Case Study: Healing a City's Trafficking Problem

Two cities having populations equivalent to Chicago and Dallas respectively, were human trafficking thoroughfares. This region as a whole had been called one of the world's poisonous hubs of human trafficking. Traffickers deceive unsuspecting parents by promising to get their daughter "married" for an affordable dowry. The proposition is hard to turn down since families often go deeply into debt to come up with the money demanded by a potential suitor. But in fact they unwittingly give their daughter's hand—and body—to an imposter who is not a husband but a criminal. The "bride" is taken across the nearby national border where neither her relatives nor her nation's law enforcement can trace her. Instead of starting a happy home, she is cast into a brothel and tortured until she submits to being a sex toy for multiple customers a day.

We Ignite Nations' (WIN)'s local leaders had, for many years, watched this kind of tragedy occur. They intervened when possible but yearned for the ability to do more. Ample laws against human trafficking existed, and the civic leaders had encouraged law enforcement to work diligently at stopping it. However, most of the police did not know how to address the problem. Some who wanted to take action feared personal repercussions from the mafia. Some enjoyed the money they were paid by the brothels to look the other way. A few were even customers themselves.

The nation ranked among the ten worst in the world for persecution of Christians. Freedom of religion was restricted, and pastors were often dragged from their churches, beaten, and thrown in jail. Therefore, Christians, churches, and Christian nonprofit organizations viewed the authorities as a potential threat and avoided them as much as possible. Keeping to their own circles, they were little known by the wider community.

The civic leaders considered the Christian organizations to be at best providers of education, medical aid, and charity to those whom society despised. At worst, they were viewed as disruptors of social order and importers of a foreign faith.

One Christmas Areef, WIN's key leader in that region, observed, "At the time of Jesus' birth, not only shepherds but also kings visited him. Jesus came for all people, so how might we as Christians show his love for our civic leaders? Let us throw a Christmas party especially for the leaders of our city!"

"You're crazy," other Christian leaders said. "You are going to expose yourself. They will misunderstand your intentions and persecute you."

But Areef persisted in his vision.

When the big day arrived, motorcades rolled up to the five-star hotel where we had arranged the banquet. Officers flanked by armed guards filed in. At the conclusion of the dinner, our children's home kids performed Christmas songs and dances, and the eldest bishop of the city gave a brief message. Then Came time for the Christmas gifts. Each leader graciously received a copy of the Bible in their native language. We prayed for them and blessed them. Some kissed the Bible as they received it, and others said, "we didn't know the Bible was available in our language!" They said, "now we know the Christians serve a God of love, because you have finally reached out to us."

Good relationships with the civic leaders were born, and a few years later, Areef was voted in as chief of twelve villages. He served his term with honesty, demonstrating biblical principles within a largely corrupt society. He utilized the government funding to improve the roads and to establish fishponds by which the villagers could generate increased revenues. All of this laid a foundation for what would happen next.

After months of prayer, study, and planning, the funding for WIN's anti-trafficking initiative became available and the project went into action. Our native team operated on four fronts: raising awareness through events and a travelling drama team, training law enforcement, spying out the brothels then busting them in collaboration with the police, and operating a safe home where we nurtured victims back into a normal healthy life.

Radhika is one of the precious lives that were saved. She was completing her college degree, pursuing her dream to become a beautician. One day on her way home she was abducted. The trafficker/pimp kept her in his house which doubled as a brothel, where Radhika was used by him and his friends and clients. When she resisted, he beat her or cut her with a knife. Her existence became a living hell, and she lost hope of ever being rescued.

But through undercover research WIN's anti-trafficking team gained intelligence into her situation. The day came when WIN guided the police to the site. The trafficker was arrested, and Radhika was rescued along with several other girls who were being kept there as slaves.

Our work cut off a major pandemic that had brought shame to the city. WIN had used wisdom, invested our resources, and genuinely impacted a serious problem that the city had been unable to solve. Moreover, we had not done it independently nor exclusively in accord with other Christian agencies. Areef and his team had initiated collaboration with the very authorities that had viewed Christians unfavorably.

The city leaders soon noticed this and summoned Areef and our anti-trafficking team to a town hall meeting. There they publicly honored us for our work in serving the city.

WIN's leaders could have said, "We Christians only do spiritual work and anti-trafficking isn't spiritual." But instead, we allowed Jesus to build ekklesia, using us—in Jesus' name and as unashamed Christian—to rescue innocent victims and bring his kingdom into an area of deep darkness. We didn't operate in the manipulative dualism that secretly says, "I'm going to help you physically but what I really want is an opportunity to preach to you." Because we saw the whole picture, the complete good news, we could genuinely love as Christ loved. In this case, it was sufficient that everyone knew we were Christians. They knew the source and origin of our love.

Girls enslaved in an earthly hell received "good news" by being freed, saved physically. Then as we mentored them, they also received the good news spiritually. The girls were discipled into hope and a new life that included not only spiritual wholeness but also physical skills training and job placement.

The police force was also "discipled;" it was empowered to bring about righteousness, and many hearts were opened to Christ. And the city itself was being discipled; it was purged of a besetting and shameful evil. An expression of God's kingdom had been unleashed, defeating the powers of darkness, healing the citywide pandemic of trafficking.

❧ ⋅✦⋅ ☙

Today our experience of Christ is not as kingly as it was meant to be. We're not Band-Aid applicators but real solutionists and problem solvers. As imago dei, the image of our Creator, we are to create and invent new things, taking what God made and stewarding and cultivating it into forms of usefulness and beauty, expression and resourcefulness, industry, and freedom. We are to be leaders taking the world into the higher way, privileged to represent King Jesus as examples to people, cities, and nations. The citizens of Christ's kingdom are destined to be healers, ambassadors of hope, guardians of life, and messengers of deliverance to a world overrun by pandemics.

When we allow Jesus to build his ekklesia, to take us into our secret calling as his healers of earth's pandemic, incredible things happen, like the following amazing account of how hundreds of families and single moms were transformed from hopelessly enslaved to welfare, to joyously employed and empowered.

8

CASE STUDY - WELFARE TO WELL-BEING

> *"Teach them his decrees and instructions, and show them the way they are to live and how they are to behave."*
> —Exod. 18:20

> *"See, I am doing a new thing! Now it springs up; do you not perceive it? I am making a way in the wilderness and streams in the wasteland."*
> —Isa. 43:19

Hug the Gunman

"I'm &#%@ gonna blow your guts out!" The raving wild man stood only a few yards away, pistol leveled at Tony's midsection. Having grown up on the streets and for some years dumpster-dove to feed his family, Tony had seen plenty of poverty, drug dealing, and crime. But this was the first time he'd found himself on the receiving end of a pistol.

With his agitation level increasing, the addict might fire at any second. His finger trembled on the trigger as obscenities and spittle flew from his lips.

Heart pounding in his throat, Tony reached out to the Lord with a quick and desperate prayer. The Lord answered, but not in the way Tony had hoped.

The still small voice of the Holy Spirit said, "Walk up to him and give him a hug."

"What?" Tony wondered if he had heard the Lord correctly. He wanted the man to put the gun down . . . from a distance! He had hoped for a miracle, like maybe that the man would see Tony's guardian angel and turn around and run. But walk toward him? While he was this irate, while the gun was still poised to blast a hole through Tony's heart? It violated common sense. The four-inch-long steel tunnel still leveled at Tony's center mass could at any second become the passageway for the lead that ended his earthly life. Tony resisted the temptation to fixate on the thought of a bullet ripping through his heart.

"Go up to him and give him a hug," the Lord said again.

Against all his instincts, Tony took a step toward the man, who waved the weapon and screamed, "I mean it! Get back! I'm gonna kill you!"

"Hey man, you're not gonna shoot anybody today," Tony heard himself say. "God has a plan and a purpose for you. Tell me, how long's it been since somebody hugged you?"

The man made a face. "What the $%@&* you talking about? Why would anybody $%@&* wanna hug a dirty homeless rat?"

Tony took another step forward. "My name's Tony. What's your name?"

The man's nostrils flared. He still kept the gun leveled. "Bill. Name's Bill."

"Good to meet you, Bill. God made you, Bill, and he loves you." Tony moved toward Bill. "And he just spoke to me, and I want to give you a hug, man. Is that okay?"

Bill lowered the weapon. Tony put his arms around the homeless addict's dirt-matted shoulders. "You're no rat. You're a precious son made in God's image, and he wants to give you hope."

Bill dropped the gun and began to weep. Tony gave him some money for food, and that evening Bill came to Tony's church.

De-Incorporated and Defamed

Though incorporated as a city in 1773, three years later Bakersfield was de-incorporated in order to oust the overbearing city marshal. For the next twenty-two years, geopolitically, the community did not exist. This lack of identity contributed to its brokenness later on. The city was reincorporated in 1898.

Situated two and a half hours north of Los Angeles, Bakersfield occupies the southern end of the San Joaquin Valley. Locally generated pollution from refineries and pesticides from agriculture, as well as smog from other areas of California, all settle in the valley. In the 1950s and '60s a well-known comedian came to town, and during his show he declared that Bakersfield stinks and it's the armpit of California. Words have power. That's why the Bible so clearly tells us not to curse but to bless.

As Jesus wept over Jerusalem, so I believe he mourns over cities and nations that languish under the rampages of the kingdom of darkness. But he desires to rejoice over those same communities if only his people perceive their high calling. So far Bakersfield had contained more darkness than light. Its historical de-incorporation and poor management combined with the negative words spoken over it culminated in an orphan spirit.

2009: Mentoring for Life

Tony and his wife, Jessica, came to Bakersfield in 2009, answering God's summons to "train, equip, mobilize, and release the church to reach the lost and fulfill their destiny to transform every aspect of society through the power of the Holy Spirit."[1] They had thought God was bringing them here to revive the churches. They had looked forward to holding revival meetings in which the Holy Spirit would reveal Jesus through signs and wonders. But as Tony puts it, they soon realized that "the whole city needed revived." As of 2010 the suburban poverty rate of Bakersfield ranked fourth worst in the entire USA, with 22.6 percent of residents subsisting below the poverty line. Soaring crime, drug addiction, and homelessness bore evidence to the community's blighted and marginalized situation. In the city's Southgate area where they chose to establish the church, there weren't even any streetlights.

Tony and Jessica started Renaissance International with Sunday evening meetings. Each Sunday morning they went out and provided free services in the neighborhood, cleaning up people's yards and engaging in random acts of love, then inviting them to church that evening. Gangs ruled the community and posed a threat to anyone who didn't blend in. One woman, however, had garnered respect, and her property was considered a "neutral zone." So whenever a gang threatened Tony's team, they swiftly made their way to her property, where they were safe!

The churches of Bakersfield had a heart for the city but didn't know how to help, apart from providing Thanksgiving and Christmas dinners to the homeless. The Lord led Tony to three churches that had indicated interest in serving the city. He also reached out relationally to the mayor and other civic officers. When the Kern County director of Health and Human Services heard that a local pastor had asked to meet with him, he was intrigued. After introductions, Tony asked, "What are the primary problems right now in our county?"

"We're facing so many problems," admitted the DHS officer. "But here's the one that's most pressing: thousands of families are on welfare. Many are recovering from substance abuse and others have felony records, so they're considered unemployable. And as you may know, TANF has been passed, which limits welfare benefits to a maximum of five years. But some of these families have been subsisting on welfare for twenty to thirty years. Now they are panicking. Soon they could all be on the streets."

"So the clock is ticking for all those people," observed Tony.

"Yes," said the officer. Leaning forward, he asked, "Can you help?"

"We will try," said Tony. "Let me pray and also talk to some of my friends. I'll get back to you soon."

The Lord gave Tony a vision and a strategy. Two friends joined the initiative: a pastor whom we will call John, described by Tony as "brilliant" and someone who had been Tony's mentor; and an excellent administrator whom we will call Becky. They established a nonprofit organization called Family to Family Mentoring (FFM). Then they developed an assessment to determine each person's needs, along with a curriculum. The curriculum included five components: Life Skills, Building Healthy Relationships, Budgeting and Financial Literacy, Career Development, and Building Healthy Social Networks. The sessions were taught in a small-group environment.

But in order to bring real, lasting healing to troubled families, many people must join the vision. So Tony stood up in front of the three church communities in the area and motivated them to intervene and help the desperate families in their county. Many believers volunteered to serve as mentors. When all the pieces were in place, Tony called the DHS officer back. "We're ready to launch a six-month mentoring program," he said. "Are there any particular families you'd like us to begin with?"

The DHS connected FFM with ten families who were soon going to lose their welfare benefits and issued FFM a grant of $10,000 to help defer costs. Tony's team visited each family and conducted the assessment. They found some of them subsisting in dilapidated rat-infested shacks or apartments with clothes, toys, and trash littering the filth-laden carpet. They found crack and cocaine, poor hygiene, obesity due to poor eating habits, unkempt children running wild and parents sprawled in front of an ever-blasting TV to drown out what they perceived as a hopeless reality.

The six-month mentoring program began. Adults committed to participate in groups of three to four families, meeting at least once a week for a couple of hours. Some met at churches, others in restaurants or coffee shops, others in parks. Each group had two or three mentors—believers who volunteered their time and skills.

Through the mentors, the participants received the course curriculum and also heard the gospel in a natural, relational way. They were inspired by the lives of the Christian mentors who also invited them to church.

The training was designed not just to provide skills and new habits that would enable formerly unemployable people to seek employment; Tony's team also created wraparound services for each module. They assisted participants to land a job . . . and not just any job! In the process of the training, the mentors learned what the participant was passionate about and then helped them get started on a path that could lead to their dream job.

By the end of the program, people who had not been employed for years or who had never gotten jobs were now earning an income that would enable them to thrive without welfare. The pilot project had experienced a whopping 80 percent success rate!

From Street Bum to Secretary and Businessman

After being shocked by the outlandish and courageous demonstration of Christ's love when Tony gave him a hug, Bill came to church. He apologized for threatening Tony's life and admitted to having been high on drugs. He lamented having nowhere to live and asked for a tent, a pillow, shoes, and a place to camp.

Tony and the Renaissance team provided the items and then allowed Bill to pitch his tent on a grassy area behind the church facility.

The following week Bill came to Sunday service and said, "In the night somebody tried to break into the church. I fought him and ran him off the property. Can I become your security guard?" So Tony's team gave him a job. Bill became a follower of Christ, and his life began to change. Sometimes he came forward weeping during the offering and put in a penny. "This is all I have now," he said, "But one day I'll be able to give more and help people as you all have helped me."

Bill went through a rehab program and became drug free. Tony's team asked him, "What's your dream?" He said he loved to work on cars, so they helped him get certified as a mechanic. Soon afterward, Renaissance moved to another building and lost touch with Bill.

Almost ten years later a man came into the church and greeted the leaders. They didn't recognize him. With a radiant smile he said, "I'm Bill! I wanted to stop by and say thank you. Now I have become a businessman. I'm running my own repair shop. Now I can give back to my community."

Olivia was one of the single moms helped by FFM. She was addicted to drugs, and her two children were not attending school. Endeavoring to get her life straightened out, she enrolled in one of the FFM mentoring groups and started sending her kids to school. She got plugged into church and came to Christ. Olivia did so well at applying the FFM lessons to her life that she soon became drug free. Her kids who used to score Ds and Fs became A and B students.

Seeing her transformation, Renaissance hired her as the church receptionist. Her ex-husband and she remarried. Now her daughter is going to college.

Olivia and Bill are only two of many complete life- and family-transformations that occurred through FFM in Bakersfield.

2011–2014: Sixteen Hours to Transformation

Upon seeing the incredible restoration of eight of the ten families, the DHS eagerly connected FFM with a hundred families and issued a grant of $100,000. To serve more people FFM dialed the mentoring program down from six months to eight weeks duration. They developed a motto: "Sixteen hours of your life can change your family forever. Will you give us sixteen hours?"

Tony and his team now realized this was way bigger than he, his two comrades, and their three churches could handle. So they started meeting with other pastors throughout the city. The leaders of FFM conducted many, many meetings. They convened small groups of pastors in which they taught and built trust and a bridge between the formerly secluded faith community and the rest of society. In 2001 and 2002, 111 churches signed a memorandum of understanding. As the united church of Kern County, they covenanted to work together to eradicate poverty in partnership with FFM.

The next question to be addressed was how, practically, should the churches work together? FFM leaders challenged the 111 churches to motivate at least one person from their congregation to volunteer to be a mentor. Some churches didn't just provide volunteers but even hosted an

FFM group themselves as one of their regular cell groups. Some mentors mobilized other mentors.

At the climax of the initiative, there were 153 mentoring groups meeting weekly. Fifteen percent of them were second generation, in which mentors had developed other mentors who'd started more groups.

As a follow-up to the mentoring, FFM identified potential services that could be provided to the families, such as food, clothing, car repair, handyman services, roof repair—over a hundred items were on the list! They put all these services onto a survey form, and local churches, businesses, and individual service providers checked the boxes next to which services they could or would be willing to provide. The data was then digitized and grouped by zip codes throughout the county. From then on, whenever a family called saying, "My washing machine is broken" or "My roof is leaking," FFM was able to guide them to a service provider that could help them.

Many single moms had no car and no way of earning enough money to buy one. This prevented them from ever being employed and made their slavery to poverty inescapable. FFM saw a solution. They encouraged people to donate their old cars to FFM, then paid for the parts to repair them. Mechanics did the work pro bono. Soon the old cars purred to life. When single moms completed the curriculum and got a job, FFM gave them a car of their own. This provided both reward for hard work and commitment, as well as incentive to continue their climb into wholeness.

Funding from government grants facilitated the training of the volunteer mentors, provided stipends and travel expenses for mentors and trainers who taught and oversaw the mentoring groups, and allowed 10 percent for administration. Some of the funds also helped participants with their first and last rent payments and with car repairs.

In all, 610 families participated in the FFM program, which achieved an incredible 78 percent success rate. Additionally, two hundred of the families started going to church and many became followers of Christ. The government officers and caseworkers recognized the massive breakthrough achieved by the collaborative work of the churches. Some of them, too, chose to follow Christ, including the assistant to the director of Human Services who testified, "I had a spiritual awakening through this process."

Along with the mentoring for families, Tony's team created POMP, the Police Officers Mentoring Program. Local police officers and the California Highway Patrol mentored troubled teens and gang members. Young people who were formerly on their way to becoming criminals and addicts instead found hope and received skills training and jobs.

Seeing the power of the church to bring good into the community, the civic leaders started directly engaging with the churches, providing funding to serve the community through other initiatives and projects. This opened the way for many more people to also hear and receive the message of Christ.

The Solution Goes Viral

Bakersfield's Southgate area was no longer dark, but streetlights weren't the only newly installed illumination. Those on welfare who desired to stand on their own feet and rise up out of poverty could now do so. They had access to a proven method by which the cycle of dependency and dysfunction could be broken. An impossible dilemma that had kept Bakersfield and other cities enslaved in a cycle of crime, addiction, and homelessness now had a solution.

Bakersfield's mayor has a strong faith in Christ and is a gift to the city. God has positioned her to change the reputation of the city and is using her to bring further transformation. She's now also the president of FFM and is taking the organization further based on the foundation that Tony and his team laid.

Word spread of the incredible transformation of lives occurring across Bakersfield's low-income community. The University of South Carolina named the program "a promising practice" and Baylor University conducted a report on it. Students came from various universities to study what was happening and to write about it as a model of transformation. Others came to learn from and replicate it.

In 2005 the Faith-Based Initiatives Office of the White House summoned Tony to Washington where he presented the project. From that time on, Tony and John received many invitations to speak and to engage in strategic planning, helping others apply the model. Out of this Tony became a cofounder of National Intermediaries, and using the FFM curriculum, he founded and currently leads Roar Academy and Renaissance Business Network.

⇾ ·✦· ⇽

What if the de-fragmented, complete good news of God's good will were done throughout the earth? What if the good King's citizens and their assemblies functioned in our full identity as his legislative body, heralds of good, solvers of problems, ensigns pointing the way to that peace which encompasses, permeates, and releases life into all areas of existence, all the while unashamedly testifying to the source of our love, the source of our courage to stand, the source of everything good—our Lord and King, Jesus? The world would look entirely different from what it does now. It would be far more joyful, far less painful. And the King could return much sooner.

PART II

UNLEASH GOD'S HIGHEST PURPOSE

"Your kingdom come, your will be done on earth, as it is in heaven."

—Matt. 6:10

"These who have turned the world upside down have come here too."

—Acts 17:6 (NKJV)

"The two greatest hungers in the world are for authentic, life-changing faith on the one hand and social justice on the other. The connection between these is one the world is waiting for."

—David Kinnaman, Barna Group

9

YOUR SECRET POWER

"I will give you every place where you set your foot . . . Be strong and courageous. Do not be afraid; do not be discouraged, for the LORD your God will be with you wherever you go."

—Josh. 1:3, 9

"The government will be on his shoulders."

—Isa. 9:6

From the previous chapters we know that Jesus has promised to build not a religious institution, not only a heaven-bound fellowship of the redeemed, but an intentional, active, powerful legislative body of his kingdom. The church is to be not just a community of faith but the living hands and feet of the Great Father Physician administering his healing balm to a broken world.

But do we really have the power to change the world? Looking out at all the evil, all the pain, all the pandemics ravaging our world causes us to sometimes just wish Jesus would come back and make it all right. That time will come. But we are alive in this world right now for a purpose.

Now is the time to make a difference, to bring healing, to shine in the darkness, to allow ourselves to be seasoning wherever we taste blandness, preservers of good threatened by corruption, and purifiers wherever we smell rot. And when we do that, a miraculous explosion of God's love and power will burst forth like nothing ever seen before.

How do we know this? Because Jesus promised to build not a synagogue, not church as we know it, but ekklesia . . . and then he added, "the gates of Hades shall not prevail against it" (Matt. 16:18 NKJV). Here is another hidden key!

Gates as Entry Points

In our modern world a gate is a point of entry or exit, or a barrier to contain or repel. As an equestrian, I know how important it is to make sure gates are closed. If a gate is left open, a horse may end up on the highway and be hit by a car.

Entry points are very important. In ancient times cities were walled and the chosen target of invading armies was the city's gate. They might burn it with fire, bash it down with battering rams, or block it to prevent anyone inside from obtaining food, thus starving the city's inhabitants until they surrendered. If a besieged city could keep their gate from being breached, they were more likely to fend off the attack and preserve their kingdom.

The gate represented a barrier between purity inside and corruption outside. Criminals were executed outside the gate (Heb. 13:12). When Jesus verbalized "the gates of Hades will not prevail" against his citizen community, he was at that very moment in the town of Caesarea Philippi, the place where ancient Israel had allowed sin to enter, leading to their downfall (Judg. 18). Like Adam and Eve in the garden, they had not kept guard and sin got in through the "gate" of their heart. The resulting pandemic of war and deportation culminated in the temporary "death" of the nation of Israel at the hands of Babylon. The most important step in restoring a city involved rebuilding the gates (Neh. 6:1).

Sin is the gateway to death. Death is the product of the sin pandemic. At Caesarea Philippi there was a physical place known as the Gates of Hades. This gaping cavern was believed to be the entry point to the domain of the dead.

Thus, "the gates of Hades will not prevail" means, in its most basic interpretation, that those who die having trusted Jesus for salvation will not suffer the "second death," eternal torment in total separation from God's presence and goodness (Rev. 21:8). Instead, they will be resurrected to eternal and glorious life. Yes! Hallelujah! "For the wages of sin is death, but the gift of God is eternal life in Christ Jesus our Lord" (Rom. 6:23).

Shortly after his journey to Caesarea Philippi, Jesus gave his life on the cross and rose from the dead, securing once for all victory over the gates of Hades, the power and reign of death. The government of death cannot hold the prince of life (Acts 2:24)! The rampage of the pandemic of evil and death was legally removed from its place of usurped authority when Jesus prevailed over sin, the gates, the entry point of death. Thenceforth, whoever believes has "crossed over from death to life" (John 5:24).

"The gates of Hades will not prevail" also means no opposing powers will be able to overcome Christ's church. Believers have suffered intense opposition—an estimated seventy million martyrs, including nearly a million in each of the last two decades.[1] Nevertheless, neither human persecution nor hell's principalities can defeat or obliterate Christ's kingdom citizenship.

These truths are foundational, but they stop short of their full glory. Jesus did not intend to leave his people on the defensive trying to repel enemy darts. A defensive and ethereal after-death interpretation of Jesus' resurrection victory has played a major role in spawning Evangelical escapism—a largely reticent and reclusive heaven-focused and earth-abjuring anti-culture that denies the power of the cross.

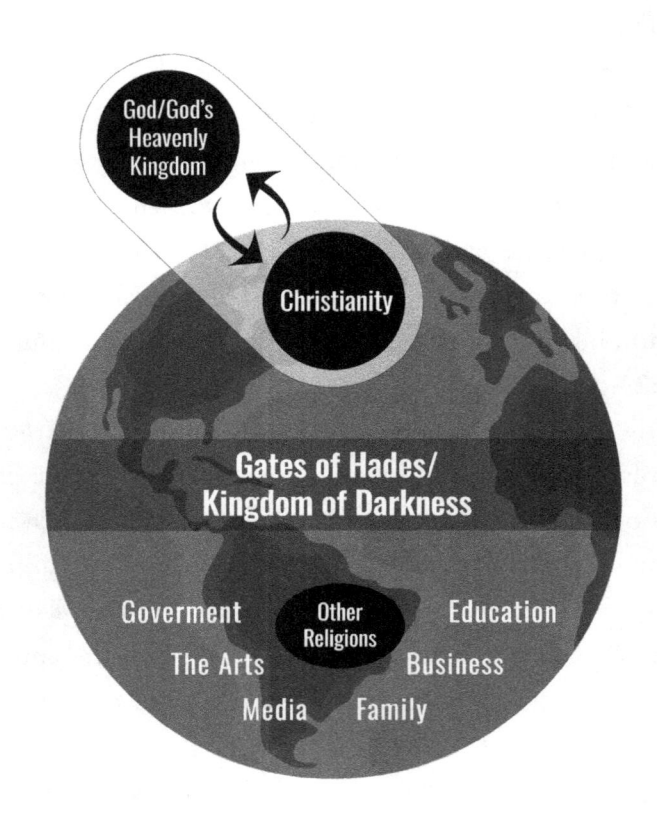

[Diagram: A globe labeled "Gates of Hades/Kingdom of Darkness" contains "Goverment", "Other Religions", "Education", "The Arts", "Business", "Media", "Family". Above/overlapping the globe are two circles: "God/God's Heavenly Kingdom" and "Christianity", connected by arrows.]

The above diagram illustrates the incomplete view: everything belongs to the kingdom of darkness and is hopelessly immersed therein. Believers are a segregated religious community, safely saved but otherwise on the defensive, waiting to go to heaven with little sense of responsibility or ability to influence this life.

"The gates of hell will not prevail" was never intended to position Christ's community as besieged victims walled up inside the safe haven of their church buildings or dangling over the edge of a cliff clinging to the safety rope of salvation while voracious demons nip at the heels of those who descend too near the vile and polluted world below. To see this passage as purely or even primarily defensive doesn't honor the context or the testimony of other scriptures. Why? Because Jesus' victory was not limited to the afterlife alone or to the unseen dimension. How do we know this? Because in the time of Christ, "gates" had another meaning as well. Here comes another secret!

Gates as Governments

Ancient cities were surrounded by walls so thick that chariots could be driven along the top. Cities therefore had both an outer and an inner gate. The area between these gates, and also any geography in the general vicinity of this entryway into the city, was called "the gates." The focal point of the city's government, as well as its commerce, revolved around the gate or gates. Prophets (1 Sam. 9:18; Jer. 7:2), the king's officers (Dan. 2:49), and kings (2 Sam. 19:8) all sat "in the gate." Men of influence came to the gate to conduct business (Ruth 4:1). The elders' absence from the gate indicated a city's decline (Lam. 5:14). Some interpret Ezekiel 43 to mean that when Christ returns, he will enter Jerusalem through the eastern gate. People are admonished to "hate evil, love good; establish justice in the gate" (Amos 5:15).

The city of God has twelve gates signifying the perfection of government, a thing often corrupted and misused across the ages of human history. Warmongering and oppressive regimes have caused so much pain and death. But the twelve gates of God's city declare that at last the good King rules, offering perfect shalom (Ezek. 48; Rev. 21).

Therefore, in the Bible, gates can be synonymous with government or rulership. For example, "Your seed shall possess the gate of their enemies" doesn't imply that Abraham's grandsons would go raid a neighboring city, rip the gate off its hinges, and carry it home to add to their antique collection (Gen. 22:17 NASB). He was saying that Abraham's descendants would occupy territory currently claimed by God's enemies. They would rule over those enemies.

Remember the commission given to the man and woman in the garden of Eden: "Rule over" the earth (Gen. 1:26). The Father King's human regents were tasked with stewardship, occupying the gates of the earth, guiding all that happened there into alignment with God's will. When Jesus builds ekklesia, he is establishing the gates—the stewardship—of his kingdom on earth.

> For the believer, "possess the gate" refers to bringing God's salvation, goodness, and healing to bear in place of the enemy's destruction and oppression.

Our traditional interpretation of the gates of Hades passage has been defensive. It perceives the church like a besieged city and the devil battering at the walls trying to break in. Victory is largely postmortem; when believers die, they will not go to hell but will have eternal life.

But this is absolutely not what is being said! The death pandemic, the reign of evil, will not be able to withstand the advance of Jesus' powerful community of love and healing, the ekklesia. It is the gates, the government of darkness that is on the defensive! It is Christ's ekklesia, his kingdom citizens, that are raiding the devil's fortress, rescuing captives, transforming lives from hopelessness to joy and welcoming myriads into the freedom of God's kingdom of light.

So when Jesus says, "The gates of Hades will not prevail" against His ekklesia, it has monumental connotations! His kingdom citizens and the legislative influence of their assembled stewardship of the city and land will drive back that which pertains to the workings of death. By proclaiming

Jesus' victory over death, death will be defeated as people enter the kingdom of God and inherit eternal life. But the afterlife is not the only place in which the destructive rule of death will not prevail. Jesus is King of life now as well as King of life hereafter. So his ekklesia is destined to serve notice of eviction to all that characterizes the death pandemic.

The ekklesia is bringing God's kingdom to bear against the spurious kingdom of the pandemic's spiritual archons. How? The case studies we've seen so far give us the pattern: True disciples living lives worthy of representing a holy God and a good King. United, targeted prayer. Proclaiming the cross and the resurrection of Jesus. Hosting Christ's presence through worship. Racial reconciliation. Intentional acts of repentance and incarnational discipleship of people and of society. Against such a kingdom legislature the gates of Hades cannot prevail, but instead have to yield.

God/God's Heavenly Kingdom

God's Kingdom On Earth
Redeeming influence of Ekklesia

Business   Media   Spirituality   Family
Goverment   The Arts   Education

Kingdom of Darkness
Corrupting influence of sin, evil, pandemics

> The ambassadorial witnesses of the Healer-Deliverer will enter the places held captive for centuries and liberate the slaves. Sectors and cities governed by the kingdom of death will be shifted toward the kingdom of life.

The long-obscured secret, the complete biblical truth, is this: God rules over all the earth. The devil is a trespasser, and the elements of the world are redeemable. Believers don't see themselves as a mere religion but as God's kingdom community. We are on the offensive, living a lifestyle of engagement, love, service, and outreach that redeems, delivers, and transforms, overcoming the works of darkness with light.

Transfer of Power

Before the cross, the devil had the right to the world's kingdoms. Thus, when he said to Jesus, "All this authority I will give you . . . for this has been delivered to me," he wasn't being presumptuous (Luke 4:6 NKJV). Jesus didn't say, "Devil, you're lying, you don't have the right to offer me all the kingdoms of the earth." Fact is, the devil *did* have that right. Humankind's sin had separated us from our source of life, authority, and good stewardship. This had allowed the devil, the false prince, to usurp rulership of the kingdoms of the earth. Across the ages of history, the world had become the devil's playground as he corrupted and destroyed, inciting God's beloved humans to often use their creative and administrative powers for evil. The earth was full of rampant, unhealed pandemics.

Before the resurrection "all this authority" had been delivered to the false prince. But on the other side of the resurrection, "all authority . . . in heaven and on earth" was transferred to King Jesus (Matt. 28:18)! At Jesus' return, the healing of the devil's pandemics and termination of his destructive works will be complete when Jesus "has abolished all rule and all authority and power." In that day "the last enemy that will be abolished is death" (1 Cor. 15:24, 26) and "the kingdom of the world has become the kingdom of our Lord and of his Messiah" (Rev. 11:15).

Because of the cross and resurrection, Jesus is "exalted . . . above every name" (Phil. 2:9) and God has "disarmed the powers and authorities" (Col. 2:15). The devil has no authority. He can only operate as a terrorist or a criminal. He has power because he has slaves—deceived and demoralized human beings who do his nefarious will. He has power because of sin and abuse, which open doorways for him to attack and torment people. But his legal access has been annulled. All authority belongs to its rightful owner, Jesus. Jesus is reigning *now*, and "he must reign until he has put all his enemies under his feet." (1 Cor. 15:25)

Those who have become citizens of Jesus' kingdom of life through faith in him have inherited his authority over the devil. Below is an example.

☙ ･◆･ ❧

Through a crackly mic and a speaker that only worked about 80 percent of the time, a native pastor led the congregation in song. Crowded into the tent, each person was immersed in the glorious presence of the Holy Spirit. "I worship you, Lord! You are the living God!" Tears of joy streaming down her face, a woman swathed in a pink-and-yellow dress waved her hands heavenward in worship. A man knelt, quietly murmuring his prayer. Even the children, forgetting their play and their peers, were wrapped in God's presence, little hands clasped and heads bowed.

Suddenly from outside there were shouts of alarm. Before anyone could respond, a mob of men brandishing sticks barged into the tent shouting radical religious slogans. They began to beat and abuse the worshippers as they scattered, trying to evade the flailing weapons. Soon some policemen arrived and forced the mob to stop its rampage. The crowd had grown massive because upon hearing the ruckus, gawkers had come out from the nearby houses and byways, wondering what was going on. The mob stood on one side of the area shouting the names of their gods while those believers who had stood their ground took up a position across from them, shouting, "Praise Jesus! Praise Jesus!"

At that moment two women began convulsing. Falling to the ground, their bodies twisted and squirmed like serpents, exhibiting classic demonic possession. Those nearby stepped back to avoid being kicked or hit. The womens' bangles shattered as they banged their wrists on the ground, and their hair fell in disarray about their tormented and sweat-soaked faces.

The woman in pink and yellow stepped forward. She shouted at the mob, "You think we are following a foreign god. You try to accuse us of being bribed to leave the idol worship. Let's see who is right. Let's see whose God is alive!"

The whole audience fell silent, and the policemen gave her their attention. Her eyes flashed with a holy boldness. "How shall we settle this? I'll tell you how!" She motioned to the ladies on the ground. "You pray to your gods! Pray to them and see if they can heal these ladies!"

A wave of murmurs went through the audience. The men who had participated in attacking the assembly, taking this to be a joke, began to snicker. The woman continued, "Do it! You cast the demons out of them. If your gods can't deliver them, then we'll pray to our God. We'll see whose God is real."

Hoping to make an inconspicuous exit from the premises, the mob started to retreat, but the police chief raised his hand. "Not so fast! You just stay put. I find this lady's proposition most amusing. You boys came here for some fun. This might be the best fun we've had in a long time." His beige-clad shoulders swiveled toward his officers. "What d'ya say, brothers?" The officers shouted in affirmation, and the chief pointed his stick at the mob and then at the two women on the ground. "Go ahead. Pray for them. You don't seem to like the Christian God, so let's see if your gods can help these women."

Muttering amongst themselves, the men who had participated in the attack shuffled forward and stood around the demon-possessed ladies. They recited prayers, calling upon the names of their gods. This went on for quite a while, but the ladies continued to writhe about on the ground. The men's shouting and chanting became increasingly frantic. Eventually the police chief stepped forward. "Okay, that's enough," he declared. "Now it's the Christians' turn." Sweating, embarrassed, and cursing, the mob returned to their side of the area, regretting they had ever come to this place. The pastor and several other leaders, along with the woman in pink and yellow, came and stood over the two women who still continued to writhe in torment. As all the believers prayed and stood in agreement, one of the believers raised his voice and declared, "Satan, in the name and authority of Jesus the Christ I rebuke you. Come out of them!"

There was an immediate change in the women. They stopped writhing and lay still and peaceful. Gasps of amazement rustled through the rapt audience. The believers began to quote Scripture and to declare, "By your blood, Jesus, you have set these women free. Thank you for going to the cross. Thank you, Father, for sending Jesus. Thank you for triumphing over every devil and every dark spirit. We declare these sisters free, in Jesus' name."

One of the ladies sat upright, and then the other did as well. They looked around, as if having just awakened from sleep. The lady in pink and yellow knelt beside them and helped them stand to their feet. The whole audience—except the mob—began to clap and cheer. The chief of police saw that the women had been fully delivered by the power of

Jesus. Turning on the mob, he declared, "We just saw which God is actually helping people. Now for the fun! Come on, boys!" With a smirk the police chief snatched up the mob leader's stick and began flailing him with it. His officers followed suit and thus gave the mob a good thrashing. Then the officers grabbed the mob leader and dragged him off to jail.

Have you put your faith in Jesus? If so, then you are a citizen of his kingdom and the Holy Spirit of the living and good Father God lives inside you. The victorious Deliverer who conquered death has endowed you with his authority. And that means you have power over every demon, every work of darkness. An important part of your secret calling is allowing the Holy Spirit to work through you to do exactly what he did in the New Testament: setting people free from demons and healing sicknesses.

The pandemic of death, the government of evil cannot hold back the advance of Jesus' authorized healers. Why is this so? Because not only did he declare the gates of Hades defeated; he also conveyed to his citizens the keys of the kingdom, the power to bind and loose!

The Keys

Now that we understand Jesus as King of all, Isaiah 9:6—one of the most powerful prophecies of Christ, our Deliverer—makes more sense. In Judaism as in other ancient cultures, when a rabbi, king, or magistrate was inducted into office, a key was laid on his shoulder symbolizing the bestowal of authority. "As God, our Lord governed all things from the beginning; as man, he set up a 'kingdom' which he still governs—upon the earth."[2] "The key of the house of David I will lay on his shoulder" (Isa. 22:22 NKJV).

David was the greatest king of Israel, God's prototype nation that foreshadowed his restored kingdom on earth. Jump forward to the end of the story, and we see again that Jesus holds the "key of David" (Rev. 3:7). This means that Jesus is right now governing, ruling. When he returns, then he "hands over the kingdom to God the Father after he has destroyed all dominion, authority and power. For he must reign until he has put all his enemies under his feet" (1 Cor. 15:24–25).

Right now, during the "church age," he chooses to rule through his ekklesia, the citizens of his kingdom. This is why in Matthew 16:18 Jesus promises to build His ekklesia and declares that the powers of the government of death will not be able to withstand its advance.

Then in the same breath, Jesus, upon whose shoulders rest the keys of authority, declares, "I will give you [his ekklesia] the keys of the kingdom of heaven" (Matt. 16:19). Here is an ancient key; his kingdom citizens now have authority to administrate his goodness out to the world around us. King Jesus has laid upon our shoulder the keys of the kingdom. We have been re-inaugurated, restored into royal stewardship of our God's good earth.

The Keys and the Sword

Government has two wings, both of which are ordained and blessed by God. Human government is referred to by Paul as "the sword"—the physical and temporal rule of human lawmaking bodies (Rom. 13:4). It is limited to the physical realm. The other wing is God's government, called "the keys of the kingdom." God's government is eternal and omniscient and is intended to provide the moral core out of which human society may prosper.

> The sword of human government may restrain evil externally, but the keys of God's kingdom change the heart, making way for true righteousness and peace.

God's government is spiritual but affects both realms. It heals the inner person through salvation and heart transformation. This inner healing also has an outward effect. Healed people have God's "laws . . . [written] on their hearts" (Heb. 8:10). No longer desiring to do wrong, they hate evil and desire to produce right action and just society. This phenomenon was showcased in movements such as the Great Awakenings, where crime all but disappeared as entire towns repented and turned away from sin.[3] It was the heart change ignited by the awakenings that birthed the US Constitution and lead to the abolition of slavery.

The keys of God's government have been given to his disciples, the true church (Matt. 16:19). It is the church's responsibility to wield the keys. This does not imply top-down dominionism, nor rigid legalism. Rather, the church's role is that of servant stewardship. The officers of God's government—believers, churches, and other kingdom communities—are called to show the way by lives of purity and by declaring right from wrong. "Holding forth the word of life" like a torch, we are to illuminate, by teaching and by demonstration, the path by which human society may prosper (Phil. 2:16 ASV).

> Wise human government listens to the prophetic voice of God's government and aligns with God's will of righteousness, mercy, responsible freedom, and the pursuit of peace.

The prophets of the Bible showed how God's government and human government are to interact. We perceive them as religious leaders, but they were in fact the advisors of kings. No wise king would go out to war without first inquiring of the Lord for prophetic guidance (see David in 1 Sam 23:1-3, and 2 Chron. 18 and 20). Prophets also rebuked cities and nations, guiding them to repentance and realignment with God's will (Is. 15-23, Jer. 21, Jon. 3, Amos 1-2, Matt. 11:20-24). Jesus himself spoke up about what today we would call political issues when he tactfully addressed officers and governments on various occasions (Luke 13:32; Mark 12:17; Matt. 23) and foretold the future of cities and kingdoms (Matt. 11:21). Wise human government listens to the prophetic voice of God's government and aligns with God's will of righteousness, mercy, responsible freedom, and the pursuit of peace.

When Jesus said, "Give… to Caesar what is Caesar's and to God what is God's" (Mark 12:17), he was not espousing a rigid "separation" but a right relationship. As demonstrated throughout the pages of the Bible, the church is to be the moral and prophetic voice guiding human government into alignment with the principles of righteousness, God's constitution. Meanwhile, human government is to provide the framework upon which faith can thrive.[4] When the State violates God's moral laws or the rights of the church, the church is obligated to call it out. If the church does not, then the church will forfeit both its legal rights and its divine appointment as a prophetic voice.

Mini Case Study: Covid versus the Churches

During the Covid pandemic, there was a period of time when it made both moral and medical sense to "shelter at home" and to take various precautions such as wearing a mask and dousing one's hands in sanitizer. In nearly every nation public assembly was forbidden, including church meetings. Most churches complied in respect for physical safety.

After church meetings were permitted to resume for a few months, the lockdown was reinstated, citing that people singing in close quarters could spread the virus. Simultaneously, some states discriminatorily allowed violent racial protests to continue, though these also constituted people gathering in large groups and shouting or chanting. Most church communities obediently took their services back online. But some considered the ban on in-person gatherings a violation of the First

Amendment which forbids the government from "prohibiting the free exercise" of religion. Among those who decided to resume in-person services in spite of the ban was Ché Ahn.

A Korean-American, Ché pastors Harvest Rock Church in Pasadena, California, and founded Harvest International Ministry (HIM).[5] Referring to church meetings, Pastor Ché declared, "We've been essential for 2,000 years!"[6] Obeying social distancing, masking, and sanitation directives, they invited the congregation back into the auditorium. Not long after, the city prosecutor issued Pastor Ché a letter threatening him with arrest and a one-year prison term. It not only declared that each church member could be fined $1,000 for every service they had attended, but even more shocking, the authorities reserved the right to arrest the churchgoers too! Nevertheless, the church stood firm.

Around this time, Pastor Ché and his team resolved to take a stand for the constitutional rights of Christians to freely worship together. Harvest Rock Church and HIM filed a federal lawsuit, representing 150 California churches in their network, against the state governor. Thousands of other churches still remained closed. Meanwhile, an additional six hundred Pentecostal churches, a group of Catholic churches and others courageously took a stand as well.[7] Each group sued the government, asserting their right to meet for worship. But Harvest Rock's lawsuit specifically demanded that state-level legislation be put in place protecting the rights of all churches to assemble.[8]

After a legal battle of nearly one year, in May 2021 the US Supreme Court ruled 6–3 in favor of the churches. An incredible victory had been won on behalf of religious freedom. The cherry on top was the $1.35 million settlement awarded to their attorney, Mat Staver, and his law firm, Liberty Counsel, to cover all legal fees. As a result, the ruling overturned the previous discriminatory limitations on churches in California, and it also implemented a permanent injunction that prevents the governor and any future governors from imposing church lockdowns in any circumstances, including a pandemic or other crises.[9]

Influencing freedom of religion isn't all that Pastor Ché and Harvest Rock are doing to wield the keys of Christ's good reign. Before being purchased by the church, the grand Ambassador Auditorium hosted plays, concerts, and other community functions. Harvest Rock does not turn away these events but regularly welcomes them to continue using the facility in between church activities. At the height of the lockdowns in 2020, Harvest Rock also planted five new satellite churches throughout California and saw many more people turn to Christ.

Pastor Ché and his team teach people the importance of social responsibility, including voting according to biblical principles. Thanks to the efforts of this initiative and the church body, fifty thousand people who weren't registered to vote have now registered. Seeing the urgency to take a stand for the lives of the unborn, Pastor Ché started a pro-life initiative in 2020 called 1Race4Life, and through another initiative called Revive California, continues working to reform society. This ongoing transformation takes place not only when Bible-believing Christians cast their ballots but also when they answer the call to run for political office on the local, state, or even national level.

Is the Holy Spirit inspiring you to be actively engaged in human government? Go for it! May he anoint you with the anointing of Daniel and Deborah and David. May kings find you "ten times better" in wisdom and character (Dan. 1:20). As you enter that arena, remember you wield keys that are more powerful than any human-delegated office, because your election is first and foremost by God. Walk worthy of Him who has called you and expect supernatural empowerment to image the King of kings. His highest purpose is that righteousness prevail and that because of your witness, influencers who otherwise would have remained in darkness "praise and exalt and glorify the King of heaven, because everything he does is right and all his ways are just" (Dan. 4:37).

Binding and Loosing

How does Jesus intend to heal through his elected citizen ambassadors? After Isaiah 22:22 and Rev. 3:7 declare Jesus to hold the key of David, both passages add, "What he opens no one can shut, and what he shuts no one can open." This is another way of saying "binding and loosing." In the Jewish culture, these were well-known legal terms meaning to declare certain things lawful and others illegal, thus opening or closing access to it. Jesus said, "Whatever you bind on earth will [already have been] bound in heaven, and whatever you loose on earth will [already have been] loosed in heaven" (Matt. 16:19). He repeats the same phrase two chapters over in Matthew 18:18. We, Christ's authorized representatives on the earth, are to bind and loose.

Binding and loosing aren't specifically about spiritual warfare nor about "claiming blessings." It is not license, as some have thought, to "take dominion" over other human beings. Such attitudes come from the "flesh," the carnal, pandemic-enslaved human nature. Jesus demonstrated that "whoever wants to become great among you must be your servant" (Matt. 20:26) and "made himself nothing, by taking the nature of a servant" (Phil. 2:7–8). "A servant is not greater than the master" (John 15:20). So our attitude must also be like that of Christ who "humbled himself" (Phil. 2:8).

Binding and loosing do not accomplish anything that God has not already determined or decreed. However because stewardship of God's kingdom on earth was delegated to human beings, our job of releasing or declaring legal that which God has already approved, and forbidding or declaring improper or unlawful on earth that which God has already forbidden, are extremely important. We hereby make way for his will to be done "on earth as in heaven."

How shall we know what he has allowed or forbidden? By knowing his Word, the Bible, and by being filled with his Holy Spirit (Eph. 5:18). By internalizing his Word (Ps. 119:11) and "walking by the Spirit" (Gal. 5:16), we have the heart and "mind of Christ," our King (1 Cor. 2:16). A believer who operates in injustice, corruption, or impurity does not have the mind of Christ and is walking in sin (Rom. 8:9). A believer who is walking in the Spirit walks as Adam and Eve did before the fall, in alignment with God's heart, hating sin but loving sinners, and loving righteousness (Ps. 45:7).

When the resurrected Jesus declared, "All authority in heaven and earth has been given to me," in the same breath he issued to his citizens what we call the Great Commission: "Therefore go and make disciples of all nations" (Matt. 28:18–19). The first and foremost way in which believers are to bind and loose is

> You are Father God's medic, the conduit through which he desires to release both eternal and earthly healing, deliverance and wholeness.

by opening the way for Father God to restore his lost children into his family. Living and preaching Christ crucified and risen "binds" the sin-death pandemic and "looses" its slaves, inviting them to be restored into the kingdom of light.

Therefore, preaching and demonstrating the message of salvation through faith in Jesus Christ is the foundational way we use the "keys of the kingdom" to "open" the kingdom of heaven to those who believe and "shut" it against those who choose not to receive Jesus, God's love gift (John 3:36; 1 John 5:11–12). On the day of Pentecost, Peter's preaching of Christ constituted the first act of loosing, or opening, to occur in what we call the church age, the time after Christ (Acts 2:14–40). All through the Book of Acts, we see this kind of binding and loosing in effect whenever the message of the gospel was preached, and people were ushered into the kingdom through faith.

But remember, the Bible is about healing *all* of human life, healing the whole pandemic. So, binding and loosing involves tangible things as well. For example, in Acts 15 some wanted to impose religious law upon new believers. Peter, James, and Paul didn't create doctrine but rather perceived what God already had decreed to be right and true. By declaring and affirming God's will, they bound the proposed legalism that would have corrupted the way of salvation by faith. In its place they loosed the truth and the possibility of many more lost souls becoming citizens of the kingdom of light.

When Jesus confounded those who would have stoned the woman caught in adultery, he bound the sexist discriminatory practices of the common culture that condemned the woman while letting the man, who bore equal fault, go blameless (John 8:1–11). Jesus loosed the possibility of change that would eventually, as today in nations that embrace Judeo-Christian values, grant equal rights to both sexes. Samaritans were a despised minority group. When Jesus made the Samaritan the hero of his story, he bound racial discrimination and loosed equal rights and the equal value of all human beings (Luke 10). When Jesus fed the five thousand with five loaves and three fish, he bound the spirit of poverty and loosed God's will of provision and plenty.

Why do we have "the mind of Christ," and why is it so important that by his Spirit we become true disciples, disciplining ourselves and conducting ourselves worthy of a holy and good Father (Gal. 5:24)? Because we are entrusted with earth's stewardship! We have the keys! We are his authorized representatives! We are to keep guard! So when we see something that is not in alignment with his goodness, we are expected to "bind" it both through prayer and also by taking action. Our case study "Suicide to Shalom" in chapter 6 is a good example of this. The believers "bound" the pandemic of teen suicides first through prayer, and then they "loosed" healing by being proactive. They reached out to schools, built relationships with community leaders, and promoted hope and kindness.

We are given the incredible privilege and responsibility to bind those things which are not in alignment with the heart of our good Father God and loose those things that are. This is your secret calling! In this way you unleash God's highest purpose, partnering with him to bring elements of his kingdom to earth, that his good will may be done on earth as in heaven. And in this way, the nations also see and millions more enter citizenship in the kingdom, becoming heirs of eternal life!

The next case study provides an amazing example of believers wielding their secret power—using the keys of the kingdom in collaboration with human government, binding the works of darkness, and releasing God's peace and transformation across a troubled city.

10

CASE STUDY - EVIL VERSUS THE EKKLESIA

"The Son of God appeared for this purpose, to destroy the works of the devil."
—1 John 3:8 (NASB)

"The Lord is with you, mighty warrior. . . . Go in the strength you have and save Israel."
—Judg. 6:12–15

Narco at a Traffic Light

"Narcohhhhhh! ¡Ay Dios mío!" Glancing left, the driver uttered a horrified cry. "Narco!! God save us!"

Like a bristling war mobile from a sci-fi apocalypse, thick armor plating, roughly bolted at odd angles, almost entirely obscured the Mercedes's onyx body. The dreaded *monsturo* cartel vehicle drew up beside Pastor Diego's car. But the driver couldn't go anywhere. The car was sandwiched in four lanes of traffic at a stoplight. Nevertheless, he jerked the wheel and inched to the right as other drivers did the same. Nobody dared honk, as this would increase their potential of becoming a casualty. All jockeyed toward the curb in a desperate attempt to obey the terror-enforced and unwritten rule of the Cali streets: when a cartel caravan is sighted, get off the road! If they perceive that you're in their way, you may join the ranks of the city's eighty-three daily homicide victims.

Pastor Diego reached into the backseat and clasped hands with his wife and daughter. They began to pray fervently. Throughout their years in Colombia not a day had passed without news of drug-related car bombs and street shootings. These were dark days for the town of Cali. The elected government had lost control of the city, which had been taken over by the drug cartels. The police were bullied and bribed into looking the other way. If they didn't cooperate, they were threatened with death and often killed by the narcos. The church was both demoralized and divided. Diego was president of the minister's association, but the pastors and their congregations felt like inconsequential islands buffeted by a sea of seething, rampaging evil. Indeed, each church was an island unto itself. For years jealousy, distrust, and arguments over minor doctrines had kept Evangelical leaders and congregations in a state of isolation, while a religious cold-war animosity erected a wall between Catholics and Evangelicals.

Crash! In the scuffle to get out of the way of the black caravan of monster war machines, cars slammed into each other. The traffic light had turned green, but the narco convoy didn't budge. This was not a good sign. It meant the boss was angry. Two vehicle lengths behind the lead monsturo loomed a full-on narco tank. At a word from the boss the men inside its turret could destroy anything that moved. Cars at the front of the press dared not proceed, or they risked being sprayed with bullets. Nobody dared get out of their car and run. Those unfortunate enough to have been on the road in this place at this moment in time could only await their fate.

The heavy armored door of a monsturo swung open with a creak as a black-clad gunman dropped to the ground. Slinging his weapon about in cavalier pomp, the hit man strutted forward. His face mask, a full balaclava, concealed all but his eyes, but beneath it he sported a savage grin. Murder was his living and he enjoyed it. He strode between the passenger cars, hesitating and staring into each. One glance elicited screams as the helpless people felt the sickening imminence of death, knowing they may be picked to be shot. But then he moved on and looked into another vehicle, inciting more terrorized wails.

The executioner moved toward Diego's car. "Duck down," Diego said to his wife. "No," she whispered, "unless you do too. If today is our time, let us go together to be with Jesus."

The gunman stood still in front of the car. Clutching the wheel, Diego's driver grimaced. He was shaking uncontrollably, a tear emitting from the corner of his eye. Then the gunman walked away, continuing his terrorism of each car. Beside the car that was three ahead of Diego's, the hit man stood longer than normal. While Diego's vehicle had been beside the caravan, this vehicle had been directly in front of it. Thus, it was perceived to have hindered their progress. Diego and his family watched in horror as the executioner raised his gun and the cries of the people inside the car filled the air with a sense of hopelessness. A barrage of bullets sent glass exploding and blood spattering. Sirens whined in the distance. The police were on their way but, conveniently and intentionally, too late. The narco hit man, demon-controlled eyes flashing with satisfied glee, darted back into the armored vehicle and the convoy roared away.

Infighting and Repentance

"Expulsado."

Pastor Randy stared aghast at words written on the ministers' association letterhead.

"Lo siento, Pastor. I'm sorry, Pastor," said the young man who had been sent to deliver the letter. "You've been excused from the association."

Randy sighed and shook his head. "I suppose I should have seen that coming," he reminisced over the past several years. In the early '80s Randy had been a cofounder of the association along with five other pastors. His attempt to bring Holy Spirit life and Christian unity to the churches of Cali had been met with varying degrees of disfavor. The chilly unresponsiveness of some leaders made Randy feel like he was being fed cold *frijoles*. The vehement resistance of others was like getting a mouthful of red-hot *habaneros*.

Randy had come to Cali heeding the Lord's call. His wife, Marcy, was the daughter of a Colombian ambassador. The home, situated in an upscale neighborhood, was four blocks from the hacienda of a drug lord, one of the seven kingpins of the Cali cartel that controlled 80 percent of the global cocaine market.[1] Considered the largest, richest, and most well-organized criminal organization in history, the Cali cartel exported seven hundred to a thousand tons of cocaine a year to the US and Europe alone. Bribery was its primary way of evading law enforcement. With the combined scourge of the criminal mafia that virtually ruled the nation, combined with corruption and inertia in the legal government, this resulted in a general state of terror under which the rest of the populace existed and tried to survive.

In this quagmire Randy and Marcy continued working to bring unity and to mobilize prayer among the churches of Cali. The church in general, with ritualistic services and believers whose faith manifested primarily on Sunday but went dormant the rest of the week, could be described as "dead." Randy and Marcy had urged, "We need to pray!" While they had mobilized prayer gatherings, attendance was sparse. Believers possessed little sense of responsibility for influencing life outside their own perceived spirituality. Many considered prayer to be for private commune with God but didn't understand it as a key to the healing of the city. Neither was community engagement viewed as important for a Christian. In this place, infamous for the world's worst drug trafficking and murder numbers, writing it all off as hopeless was easy.

Randy and Marcy were at their wits' end, but they kept praying for a breakthrough.

Pastor Diego woke with a start. Something was strange. He had never felt this way before. His heart felt heavy, as if a fifty-pound stone had been inserted into his chest. A chill went through him. A heart attack? He glanced at his wife, asleep. Should he wake her? He put a hand on his breast. The heaviness didn't seem physical. His heart seemed to be beating normally. What was this strange sensation? Then he realized: the heaviness was spiritual. God's presence was in the room!

"God wants to say something to me! He is here! I am in his presence!" Diego found himself kneeling on the floor beside the bed. He began to pray, "Lord, what do you want to say," but before the words passed his lips, a still small voice spoke and pierced his innermost being. "You must repent. My body is hurting. My people are hurting one another. You must repent on behalf of my people. Healing starts with humility."

The next morning Diego scheduled a special meeting of the ministers' association and sent Randy a personal invitation, hoping desperately that he would forgive and come back. He did.

At the meeting Diego told how the Lord had spoken to him. There, in the presence of all his peers, with tears in his eyes, he apologized to one after another. The grievances weren't massive, but they had earned him a reputation as being a little on the brash side. He also repented on behalf of the church of Cali. Then he went over to Randy. He asked Randy to forgive him and invited him to consider rejoining the ministers' association.

Within moments Diego watched in awe and joy as many of the leaders began to weep and to repent as well. They asked forgiveness of each other for hurtful words, jealous attitudes, and selfish ambitions, and for the Cali church as a whole. And then they all embraced each other and praised God together.

The Lord could now use his royal stewards to bring healing to the city. But to get around their still-partial vision, he would have to throw in a twist.

May 1995: The King's Court

Some of the Christian leaders decided it was time to take action to bring the gospel to Cali. What came naturally to them was to host an evangelistic crusade. They reserved the city's Colisco El Pueblo with seating for twenty-five thousand and booked a well-known Latin American evangelist. They advertised and publicized the event all over the city with fliers, phone calls, and radio ads. Everything was ready for the big night. Then only days before the event, the evangelist canceled!

The leaders held an emergency meeting. Most agreed the event must be canceled.

"We shouldn't make such a big decision as this without first praying," Randy said. "But let's not only talk to God. Let's also take time to listen. Let's ask him to show us what he wants us to do." A few pastors gave him sideways glances thinking, "The Holy Spirit pusher is back at it." But with minimal murmurs, the leaders bowed in prayer.

Eventually, Randy said, "I believe we need to proceed. We must go ahead with this meeting. What do you think about having all-night prayer and worship led by the local pastors and their churches? We don't know how many people will come, but we do know the Lord will be there, because his Word says 'where two or more gather, I am there among them.'"

Others nodded. "You're right. Let's walk by faith."

One of the women leaders likened the situation to that of the people of Israel faced with the impossibility of crossing the Red Sea but with Egyptian chariots cutting off the possibility of retreat. "This is a time to go forward, not backward," she said. "We must trust God, and maybe he will do a miracle."

On the big day, while the worship team warmed up, volunteers roped off most of the seats because only a small crowd was expected. To their shock, outside the gate people began to congregate, and when it was opened, a stream of humanity flooded into the stadium. And they kept coming! The roped-off sections were opened. When all the seats were filled, hundreds more stood outside, listening and participating as best they could.

Along with powerful worship and messages, the mayor also mounted the platform and proclaimed, "Cali belongs to Jesus Christ!" The crowd roared in affirmation, chanting in unison, *"Levanta a Jesús,* Lift Jesus up!"

When the scheduled activities had concluded, nobody wanted to leave. The meeting turned into a concerted intercessory extravaganza. People cried out in prayer on behalf of their broken and wounded city. On and on the *vigilia* went, twenty-five thousand believers in unison inviting God's "will to be done" in Cali "as it is in heaven." Fervent prayer went on all night until six the next morning.

The church in Cali had arisen from its slumber and had joined together as one in declaration of his Word and will. Until this occurred the gates of Hades, the government of death, was able to run rampant. The church in Cali had, whether consciously or not, stepped into its secret calling, activating its authority and responsibility. King Jesus' authorized guardians of Cali had engaged their kingdom keys and bound what was not an alignment with God's goodness. Now the Holy Spirit could more effectively bring about the Father's will.

For as long as anyone could remember there had never been a death-free day in Cali, which suffered the highest homicide rate in the world. But for the twenty-four hours following the united prayer rally, not a single person was killed.

The president of Colombia at that time was corrupt, and his election had been paid off by the drug cartels. Despite this, he issued an executive order sacking about three hundred Cali police officers who had been secretly collaborating with the narcos.

Up until this time, the newspapers, radio, and TV had remained silent about the problem of the drug cartels. Nothing was published or spoken of publicly for fear of retaliation. But now, God's publicity system went into action! In June several intercessors had dreams predicting that the Cali drug cartel leaders would be subdued. During a worship symposium in Bogotá, Randy received a word from the Lord that the drug lords would be exposed.

Two weeks later the Colombian government declared all-out war against the drug barons. Sixty-five hundred elite commandos descended upon Cali, and by August all seven targeted cartel leaders had been captured. A city that had been almost completely controlled by drug lords was returned to the administration of elected law and justice. Something awesome had happened in the unseen realm that had affected what happened in the natural. The streets became safe, and people no longer had to fear a violent death.

December 1995: Assassination and a New Identity

The gates of death had been driven back, but the movement was fragile. Lacking a clear picture of their identity as the ekklesia, the believers weren't sure what had happened. The Christian community possessed few models for engaging their spiritual authority to affect all realms of life. The foray into a whole-life healing adventure might quickly revert to the defensive exit-focused synagogue.

Just as fragile was the unity between the Christian leaders, which hung by a thin thread. They had collaborated to put on one grand event, which had come off far better than they had imagined. But would the ekklesia continue to work together?

The early church father Tertullian said, "The blood of the martyrs is the seed of the Church." And so it would be in Cali. In December, on his way to a prayer meeting, pastor-evangelist Julio was gunned down by members of the drug mafia. His widow was informed and called Randy. When Randy arrived at the church, he found Julio shot dead on the sidewalk.

Grieving the loss of one of the King's champions, fifteen hundred people gathered for Julio's memorial service, including Christian leaders who hadn't spoken to one another due to animosity or doctrinal feuds. These leaders declared, "Let us covenant together to walk in unity from this day forward. Let Julio's blood be the glue that binds us together in the Holy Spirit." That covenant of unity was thereafter signed by two hundred churches that committed to work collaboratively to bring Christ and his righteousness into their city.

From then on all-night prayer rallies were held every two months with large prayer extravaganzas annually. They would become Cali's famous *vigilia*. Such was the enthusiasm and passion of the believers that even the 55,000-seat Pascual Guerrero soccer stadium couldn't contain the *vigilia* participants. Latecomers simply formed their own meetings outside and circumambulated the venue, praying and praising the Lord.

The Christians of Cali discovered their secret calling. No longer were the churches embattled islands trying to keep from being washed away by evil. Instead, they were now on the offensive, driving evil out of their city. The following years were marked by strategic coordinated prayer initiatives and explosive church growth. "The Church decides the future of the nation," says Gisella Greenfield, missions leader of Cali's Christian Community of Faith Church.[2] "If the Church steps aside and says, 'That's none of our business,' the enemy will do whatever he wants. But now the Church that was dormant has woken up, stepping into our destiny to set the path and pace for the nation."

The gospel had come to be seen as practical and applicable to life circumstances. This not only resulted in a grand harvest of souls in general but also opened the door for government leaders and businesspeople to turn to Christ. The entire soccer team became citizens of Christ's kingdom. Cali's mayor and city council approached the ministerial alliance. "We want you to manage a citywide campaign to strengthen the family," said the mayor. From then on, the church enjoyed full access—without cost—to use the soccer stadium, the sports arena, and the velodrome for any seminar or prayer event that ministered to broken families. "When you humble yourself before the King of kings," said Gisella, "like Nehemiah, you receive the favor of the kings of the earth and they ask what they can do for you." The transformation spread beyond Cali to other Colombian cities and was featured in George Otis's *Transformations* video series.

But some years later, the enemy would launch a pandemic of a different sort.

2016: Repulsing a National Attack on Children

What is worse than an epidemic of drug cartels? A pandemic that destroys an entire generation, the loss of our children. A global pandemic wafted its way across the planet, originating largely in the US. This virus deceived parents into allowing institutions and the government to indoctrinate their children. It aimed to undermine parental rights while creating primary school curriculum that injected certain viewpoints into the malleable souls of innocents as young as five. This virus was loaded with unbiblical viewpoints, inoculating young minds against faith, and promoting atheistic worldviews along with fracturing identities.

The unspoken intent was to render the next generation putty in the hands of those who would exploit them. Among other evils, this virus foisted upon the children a system of belief that demanded equality without responsibility and liberty without boundaries, and purported to eliminate racism while actually promoting it. For those people wise enough to learn from the past, history confirms this anti-Christ deception had led not to equality but to slavery, not to prosperity but to poverty, and had climaxed in genocide (think Lenin, Stalin, and Hitler) or starvation (think Communism) or implosion (think the Roman Empire) in every culture and nation it infected.

This pandemic had already swept across other historically Christian nations with little resistance. By 2016 it was running rampant in the US when it invaded the shores of Colombia. But the evil one's agenda of death was about to slam smack into a mighty battalion—for the government, the gates of death cannot prevail where Jesus has built his governing body, where his ekklesia has arisen to her calling as his royal guardians!

The God-defying, soul-stealing, mind-twisting booklets were all printed and ready to go into the schools. The new curriculum that would infiltrate every school in Colombia was ready to be launched. Laws had also been passed that would restrict the rights of parents to choose which school their child attended. By all appearances nothing could stop the new legislation.

Then, all on a single day—August 10—the streets of every major city of Colombia were filled with people. Marcy, senior pastor of Cali's Christian Community of Faith, said it was supernatural. Everyone who cherished righteousness came out on the streets and declared, "We demand the right to tell our children what's right and what's wrong. The schools do not have this right." Those on the streets were not just Evangelicals. All who cared about family turned out in droves, including Catholics, Jews, and Muslims. They marched shoulder to shoulder for that which they held in common—the biblical definition of family.

The marchers wore white shirts declaring their commitment to the purity of the minds of their children. They trod the streets not in a spirit of anger or protest but as occupiers, as those having authority, as the victor saying "No!" to a vanquished foe that tries to raise its head. It was more of a worship march than a protest. People were joyful, smiling, praising God. They carried banners that declared, *"Unidos Transformando!"* meaning "United we transform."

Gisella recalled, "The Church had understood her power. She had taken up the place that she had given up for years and years." It was a real-life demonstration of the triumphant truth that we are seated with Christ in heavenly places (Eph. 2:6) and that "whatever you bind on earth will be bound in heaven" (Matt. 18:18). The marchers courageously carried forth into the physical realm what God had already decreed, the heart and will of Jesus. That day sparked a saying that is now popular throughout Colombia: *"No te metas con mis hijos!"* or "Don't mess with my kids!"

With such a massive turnout in opposition to the school curriculum, the government was compelled to listen. The atheistic minister of education who had allowed the virus to come into the nation resigned. The curriculum did not enter the schools. In fact, the church then took things further, securing legislation that protects parental rights and prevents any future imposition of ungodly curriculum in the schools. Also, parents had for many years been forbidden to homeschool their children. But now, as an outcome of the rally, the government issued blanket permission to homeschool.

Healing Human Governments

Today, one need not go to the park to bask in a tropical paradise. Just find yourself invited into Marcy's home. No longer surrounded by drug lords, the upscale neighborhood is now peaceful and safe. The center of her lovely home is intentionally open to the sky, with a palm tree growing up through the ceiling. By night, guests are serenaded to sleep by crickets and by day little birds perch in the tree and sing. Her living room and patio look out on a manicured lush green expanse adorned with tropical blooms. In the kitchen Marcy's cook prepares the most delightful *arepas* and fresh-squeezed fruit juices like the nectar of heaven. But the real treat is talking with Marcy, a Deborah in the kingdom, a stateswoman who influences governments and is honored as a counselor of nations.

After Randy passed, Marcy became the senior pastor of Christian Community of Faith Cali. But she also blossomed into a whole new dimension of influence. Today she is the president of Mission South America, a network of over ninety churches working regionally to train leaders and churches throughout Colombia and other continents. She serves on the Board of Global Council of Nations, which works with high-level global leadership and provides biblical training to presidential candidates and other national-level leaders. In 2021 six hundred lawyers, economists, pastors, and government leaders were trained by

Transforming the Nation Movement, founded by Marcy and her leaders to equip pastors and professionals with a biblical worldview.

Marcy says, "There is a spiritual hunger mantle over Colombia. It is still there today. The awakening has not stopped."

Gisella adds, "Now the police come to the church and kneel in front of the church. They say, 'As men of God, we want to do right. We need Christ and the values of the Bible. We need the church's prayers.' Whenever there is suicide or domestic violence the civic leaders come to us. 'We need the church!' they say. 'The church heals the wounds of our city that no one else can heal.'"

"We train the church," says Marcy. "But we don't stop there. We train the city. We train the nation."

What happened and is still happening through the church in Colombia can happen in any city, any nation. Marcy warns that to look for a formula is a trap. God will work differently in every situation. However, he works through his Church. Jesus desires to build his ekklesia in all its full expression, to build it in every sector of life.

⋇⋅✦⋅⋇

The foregoing chapters have revealed a series of secret keys that across the ages have lain hidden, or were misunderstood, or were only partially apprehended. You now hold these ancient keys, and can see God's highest purpose.

But how can you enter into it? The case studies have provided actionable examples, but let's now get really practical.

11

MIND SHIFTS AND THE THREE-P KEY

"The Spirit of the Lord is upon me, because he has anointed me to preach the gospel to the poor; he has sent me to heal the brokenhearted, to proclaim liberty to the captives and recovery of sight to the blind, to set at liberty those who are oppressed; to proclaim the acceptable year of the Lord."

—Luke 4:18–19 (NKJV)

"Traditional Christian teaching has been otherworldly in its emphasis. It has had more to say about how to accept failure than about how to succeed, more about suffering than about action."

—Lesslie Newbigin

Your secret calling is to be an ambassador of God's goodness. An ambassador is a royal steward authorized to represent the king, president, or prime minister. As such, an ambassador must be clear about their royal assignment and also must know the king intimately so as to fully and accurately represent him. This is why the initial chapters were essential—to deliver us from our partial understanding of God and our shrunken view of ourselves.

The ambassador brings the king's goodness into a foreign land where that goodness may not currently be in effect. Likewise, as delegated stewards of the earth but citizens of God's kingdom, we bring his kingdom into every sector of life.

Ambassadorship in the court of the King of kings is a lofty post! How big is God? Big! Powerful! Because he chooses to work through humans, he wants to be big and powerful through you!

Many believers are like frustrated pilots driving their airplane round and round on a taxiway wondering why they can't get airborne. It is because their airport—their worldview, their view of God and of themselves—consists of a skewed and incomplete framework. The taxiway goes in circles but never permits liftoff because they haven't seen the whole picture of who God is and who he has called them to be.

The endless taxiway is about to open up onto the runway! First of all, you are no longer going to continue in the same vicious circle of brokenness or depression or frustration. You're going to walk in freedom and be launched into influence. How? I am challenging you to allow the following teachings to reform your paradigm and worldview around truth instead of half-truth.

Secondly, how can you individually and your church community corporately enter what you knew deep down existed and at last have a framework for, i.e., a faith that redeems and changes the world instead of hiding from it? How can you fulfill your long-concealed appointment and purpose as Jesus' soul-saving, pandemic-healing, value-creating, goodness-guarding ambassador?

In order to live out your secret calling, some mind-set resets and paradigm shifts may be in store.

From Pitfalls to Platforms

Abuse, addiction, bitterness of heart, and torment of soul are debilitating. They originate straight from the kingdom of death, the sin pandemic. But here's the secret: God's goodness will make those very things into your launch pad!

> Your past and your present are a preparation for your highest purpose.

Of course, your family, skills, education, and employment. But even the things that weren't so positive—difficult relationships, abuse, or physical or emotional challenges—all these are part of your preparation for your promotion as a legislator of God's healing grace, because he causes "all things to work together for good to those . . . who are called according to his purpose" (Rom. 8:28 NASB).

Joseph was cast into a pit, then sold as a slave . . . by his own brothers! But Joseph knew God and knew his secret calling. The pit and prison experience, and Joseph's response to it, became a platform and culminated in his promotion to a palace as vice president of what was then the most powerful nation on the planet.

Your still-open heart wounds will heal fully when you do two things: First, forgive. Refuse to act like the slave the lies say you are. Offense has no right to attach itself to you (Rom. 6:16).[1] Disallow bitterness (Heb. 12:15). It is a choice, just like love. Once you make the choice, like an infection that has been exposed and cleaned, healing can happen.

Secondly, instead of focusing on your own needs or weakness, offer what strength you have to serve the Lord and others. Joyce Meyer said, "my test became my testimony; my mess became my miracle and my message."[2] The act of giving out of your brokenness or lack allows the Great Healer to pour his healing balm into your wound (1 Kings 17:7–16; Luke 6:38). Before long it will no longer ache. And then you will see the reason for it, and finally you will plant your feet upon it and find yourself in a higher place, empowered in a way you were not previously. The chain by which you were bound to your dark yesterday will become a tow rope buoying you up into a bright tomorrow.

From Defensive to Offensive

Ten of the twelve spies who were sent to scout out the promised land returned with a defensive, self-centered, and fear-filled "the giants are too big and we're too small" report. Only two saw that God—through his people—was bigger than the giants (Num. 13). Today the ratio is often the same. Why do so many live on the defensive? Because the partial gospel leaves a knowledge gap, and lack of knowledge opens the door to fear, and fear is the antithesis of faith. We have lacked understanding that Jesus is King of all, that we are his appointed representatives. Thus, fear finds a foothold inflating the devil, our problems, and the evil in this world to look bigger than it actually is.

Knowledge empowers us with truth, and truth dispels fear.

In the same way, every believer individually, every kingdom community, and the body of Christ as a whole are intended to play offense, not defense.

> When you switch from avoidance to courage, what seems like a mere pebble becomes more powerful than Goliath's sword.

The King has given you the keys of the kingdom. They are in your hands! Declare yourself delivered from defensive living. Discover what it means to be a royal administrator of the good King, binding that which promotes the sin pandemic and loosing that which promotes healing.

From Humanism to Jesus the Rock

The novice gold miner celebrates what appears to be a million-dollar nugget… until the jeweler informs him it's nothing but fool's gold. As the path to hidden treasure is not without deceptions, likewise many have strayed into the "social gospel," emphasizing human betterment while allowing the first part of the ancient key—relationship with God—to fall by the wayside. Jesus is not declared to be the Rock but becomes merely one among many building blocks. Not only does this omit the foundational work of bringing people into kingdom citizenship, failing to rescue them from the spiritual domain of death; it also casts aside our ambassadorship, the keys of the kingdom. Instead of leveraging our royal position "seated . . . with Him" (Eph. 2:6), instead of activating the keys of the kingdom, the authority of Christ's victory over the pandemic, we lay aside God's armor and the sword of his Spirit (Eph. 6:10–18), and instead batter away at it with our weak human frailty. Impotent to create inner heart transformation, superficial appearances of change will not last. We have produced fool's gold, not the real thing. Or having done good works but omitted any connection to him, we attribute to humanism what belongs to God and thus commit idolatry.

Do not be ashamed of your King (Luke 9:26). Though you may be persecuted, the end result will be purest gold (Prov. 17:3; 1 Pet. 1:7).

Mini Case Study: Water and the Water of Life

In many remote mountainous regions, villagers languish without access to water. Among many other activities, WIN (We Ignite Nations)[3] installs permanent water systems in these communities. Believers in these regions suffer some of the world's worst persecution. Nevertheless, our native leaders ensure from the start that the villagers know we are followers of Christ. We refuse to be ashamed of the gospel.

The local pastor and his team inform us of the need and participate in the initial survey. We then facilitate a relationship between the church and the town mayor and other government representatives. These two parties, which historically have been suspicious of one another, learn that they have common interests and can work together.

WIN then begins the process of fundraising while also working with the villagers, helping them understand how much the water system will help them. With the exuberant blessing of the local government, which now recognizes that the local church has initiated this essential development, the project ensues with the local community providing most of the labor.

We also provide training in biblical values, which helps the whole community to thrive. In this way the community is "pastored" into a complete experience of Christ's healing. We aren't just providing another social development project. Nor do we have ulterior motives. We're genuinely serving human beings, bringing in an aspect of a higher way, God's will of wholeness in all aspects of life, anchored upon the one foundation, Christ.

When the system is finished, each family has year-round water piped to their doorstep. For the first time ever they have ample water not only to drink and cook food but also to bathe, irrigate their fields, and raise animals. Girls now carry school backpacks instead of heavy water cans. Mothers don't have to fast in order to feed their families, and toddlers' bellies aren't bloated from malnutrition. No longer hopeless, fathers overcome alcoholism and become breadwinners.

In and through it all, they see Christ because the work was unashamedly founded upon him and co-led by the local church community. They know that Jesus is the Water of Life (John 6:35; 7:37–38). Many more people choose to put their faith in Jesus and become vibrant disciples. The ekklesia community becomes viewed as an "essential service," and the village as a whole experiences some aspect of "on earth as in heaven."

From Dualism to Holism

As mentioned earlier, through the centuries we have been molded—often subliminally without our even realizing it—into a perspective where the elements of daily life, such as work, recreation, money, sexuality, and commerce, are external to and separated from spirituality. This dissection of the world has fed the misinterpretation of passages such as "Do not love the world or anything in the world" (1 John 2:15).

What is "the world"? What are the things "in the world" that the apostle is referring to? Is he referring to created things, or to the misuse of those things, i.e., sin? The next verse provides the answer: "the lust of the flesh, the lust of the eyes, and the pride of life" (1 John 2:16). Creation is not the pandemic. Creation is the victim. The pandemic exists in the misuse of created things, whether of our brain to think evil thoughts or our hands to do evil deeds. So the warning does not adjure us to renounce physical things but rather to keep ourselves from sin. "The flesh" is not hands and lips but rather our propensity to use them in opposition to God's goodness.

> "The world"—people with their activities and cultures and nations—is not hopelessly corrupt. It is that which "God so loved" that he sent Jesus into it to redeem it (John 3:16). And he sends us into it as well.

But our partial-gospel perspective has tragically trained us to avoid "the world" in hopes of avoiding sin.

Likewise, "Come out from them and be separate" was meant to result in separation from personal sin, not segregation from the world into which we are sent in order to bring abundant life (2 Cor. 6:17). How embarrassing to think that those destined to steward the world into heavenliness have instead quarantined ourselves from it in fear that it would steward us into worldliness! We have inadvertently locked God in a small sector called religion, banished from the rest of his creation! Let us arise from our sidelined subculture and remember that salt seasons and preserves. Light illumines. Neither blandness nor decay can overcome salt. No darkness can snuff out light. What then do we fear? What are we waiting for?

When believers engage in something that is considered political, such as campaigning for a candidate, or when we build a business to generate revenues, or when we invest in learning a skill to enter a new profession, or when we participate in a social function, many of us do so with a creeping sense of uncertainty. We ask ourselves, "Is this really important? Shouldn't I be a full-time preacher instead of pursuing a business or working a regular job?"

> The healing contagion of life that we carry will no longer be conveniently quarantined within holy huddles but joyously administered to heal a wounded world.

Some indeed are called by God to exclusively devote themselves to proclamation of the message of Christ and to be sustained thereby (1 Cor. 9:14). However, for those not thus called, the perception that the marketplace is less spiritual than the pulpit comes straight from the enemy and is just one more lie to divert you from the secret. Entrepreneurs are some of the "most strategically placed soldiers," having influence with the people and structures that shape culture and sustain life.[4] How will those in the pulpit reach those in the corporate high-rise, the military, the sports arena? Who will be Jesus to those who would otherwise never darken the doorway of a church or watch an online gospel presentation? The world has yet to see the power of "redemptive entrepreneurship"[5] on a large scale—marketplace leaders leveraging business acumen, wealth, and vision to defeat the "global giants" in the name of Christ.

Friend, the King of all has sent you into this world to model his life against the forces of death. The world around us is neither meaningless nor hopeless; it is his beloved creation, taken captive and victimized by the sin pandemic. The time will come when he will set it all free. Until then, the world cries, "Is there no balm in Gilead?" (Jer. 8:22). There is! Let us stop limiting our all-powerful Lord! Let Jesus, the Great Physician, heal you now of the mindset that keeps you from entering your secret calling, your destiny as a healer of earth's pandemic. Then let Jesus the Healer flow through you to affect healing upon whatever crosses your path.

Identify Your Promised Land

Now let's get down to business! What you're to *be* may be in sight, but on what target are you to focus? What are you called to *do*? For you specifically, what is *your* secret calling, the activity that will bring about God's highest purpose of whole-person, whole-life healing and deliverance?

First of all, if you have not yet become a citizen of the good King's kingdom of life, what are you waiting for? Choose to turn from the sin-death lifestyle and from trusting in yourself. Put your trust in Jesus who suffered and died in your place and rose up, triumphing over the sin-death curse, to give you life. Become an heir, a royal son or daughter of the King!

Secondly, your secret calling will align with the heart of God. It will not oppose or disregard God's written Word, the Bible, or his goodness. It is a summons to stand for truth, for goodness, for life, and for Christ. If some voice whispers in your mind a suggestion of something that brings harm, it's not God. It comes from the kingdom of darkness and is to be refused and rejected. God's voice will summon you to serve, empower, rescue, uplift, invent, honor, protect, build, innovate, provide solutions, oppose evil, and do it with a spirit of humility, excellence, and love for others.

There are seasons to life, and so there may be a season in which you fulfill one assignment and then a different season in which a new calling beckons. Don't regret or resist the transition. Embrace it, rejoice in the former, and anticipate with joy the new venture. Some may be given more than one secret calling to pursue simultaneously.

Identify a focused, specific target. There is a promised land for you to possess, a beauty to be rescued, a need to be met, a wrong to be righted, a truth to be lived for . . . and perhaps even a love to be died for.

The Three-P Key to Find Your Promised Land

Below is the Three-P Key to identify your promised land, the targeted focus of your secret calling.

Passion

By the age of twenty-eight Jon had lost both his younger brothers to drugs. Jon himself might have gone the same way, but his faith in Jesus helped him turn his pain into purpose. The agony of seeing his siblings murdered by drug addiction ignited Jon and propelled him to serve and rescue others who were running toward the same destruction. Leveraging his skills as a businessman, he founded an organization called Natural High.[6] He began interviewing athletes, musicians, and youth role models asking them to tell their stories, including how they find peace and stay drug free amid the pressures of competition and popularity. Many of the athletes testify of the central role their faith in Christ plays in their lives. Jon produces these incredible stories into inspiring, action-packed short videos that are shown across the United States in thousands of schools to help young people stay free from addictions and live their "natural high." This is just one of the ways Jon is living his secret calling, fulfilling God's highest purpose.

What problem, need, injustice, opportunity lies before you and cries out for you to take action? What incites you to holy anger? What ignites you with uncontainable joy? What excites you or carries a sense of urgency? What motivates you? That may be your promised land.

Preparation

"It's impossible," said the manager. "Keep 110 megawatts of power flowing through this turbine while somebody trues up the collector ring? If anything went wrong, the fire that would go through his body would melt him from the inside out. Or he could get caught in the machinery. Nobody would even be able to recognize the remains. It's way too dangerous."

"But I still think it could be possible," persisted Dave, "to make a tool that could do the truing while the generators are running. How much does it cost your company to shut down the turbines for truing?"

"A million dollars a day," replied the manager, "and sometimes it takes multiple days."

Multibladed turbo generators are powered by a stationary carbon brush that passes electrical currents to a collector ring spinning at 3,600 rpm. The surface of the ring eventually degrades and has to be "trued up," or resurfaced, so that it runs smoothly. The only way to "true up" the collector ring was to shut down the generators, incurring much expense.

At the time, Dave's company, Cutsforth Products,[7] was barely staying in the black. The big factories weren't buying his carbon brushes, but as he interacted with the managers, he noticed other machinery parts that were broken. "We're so frustrated," said the managers. "Nobody knows how to fix this stuff."

Dave was a committed Christian and believed that creativity and helping people solve everyday problems was part of glorifying God. He took seriously the needs of the factories and figured out how to make the parts they needed, even some parts that wouldn't make him much money.

But the dilemma of truing the superpowered generators ignited Dave with another kind of energy and power.

His big breakthrough came with the invention of the Truing Tool.

For many years thereafter the primary income for Cutsforth Products came from using the novel Truing Tool to service big power plants. Along with this, Dave and his wife, Marlyce, raised a beautiful family, helped start a church, and invested strategically in bringing Christ's kingdom into the most unreached ends of the earth.

Dave had six patents, but his eldest son, Rob, who now leads the business, has over a hundred! One of these inventions now generates 70 percent of the income for the business.

In churchdom we often laud a traditional minister, noting, "He is an anointed preacher" or "She has a prophetic anointing." We say a Christian musician or a particularly moving worship song is "anointed." But why are we so hesitant to thus recognize the touch of heaven upon things that aren't deemed inherently spiritual? Elijah did fourteen miracles, and Elisha's "double portion" anointing resulted in him doing twenty-eight.[8] What worlds of beauty unfold when we dare recognize that an invention is a form of miracle, for it is the Creator expressing himself through his co-creators to bring something into being that formerly did not exist. "Inventor" is a genuine anointing from the Holy Spirit, and God certainly gave a double-portion to Dave and his son.

"Creation shows forth the glory of God," says Rob. "So much understanding about him can come by way of living in and experiencing what he has made. And he lets and encourages us to 'stick our hands in it,' and be further amazed by it. God wants everything we do to be done heartily as to him. He wants to walk with us in his creation."[9]

Rob says, "I come to tears over inventing. It gives me intense joy. I feel the smile of God." Solving people's problems by inventing tools is how he fulfills the greatest commandments: loving God and loving his neighbor as himself. He has found that faith expresses itself in work and creativity. This complete experience of the goodness of God is for Rob the most fulfilling and powerful act of worship.

What are you uniquely equipped to influence? It may not be your passion, but it's where you've been placed, what you've been prepared for. You may be called to "bloom where you're planted." Your skills and abilities enable you to solve a problem, fulfill a role, generate a breakthrough, or multiply a successful model. Life's hardships can be the best source of preparation. Don't waste your pain. Allow it to give you a testimony, to prepare you to heal others. Your promised land may well be none other than that for which life has prepared you.

Protest

Your promised land may be the very thing you've been running away from or resisting! The thing that when the thought crosses your mind, you protest and cry "Noooo!!! Not me! Don't send me there!" or "I don't want to do that!" Just remember, most heroes become so unwillingly. Jonah did not want to go to Nineveh, but after God eventually got him there, the city was saved.

I was twenty-three years old when the Lord called me to go to the opposite side of the world. I did not want to go! I said, "Anywhere but that place!" But then he gave me a supernatural love for a place and a people that I previously considered the most unattractive piece of geography on earth. He then gave me a strategy, and he led me to the people who could bring his highest purpose to pass. I found myself a tool in his hand to bring hope and healing to a land that had been without his love for millennia. My protest when surrendered to his purpose prepared the pathway to praise. And that ambassadorship against which I had protested is now one of my most prized passions!

As the good Father's beloved son or daughter, you may be called to discover and implement a way to end human trafficking in your city or to educate and nourish children through sustainable innovations. You may be called to bring unity to fractured groups or promote peace between rivals. Your entire primary calling may be the direct verbal proclamation of Christ, the way of salvation for all who believe.

As the Creator's deputy scientist or engineer, you may be called to create something that revolutionizes the entire world, as did the combustion engine and the microchip. You may be the next athlete to set a new world record or the next musician to develop a moving piece of music.

As a royal steward to the King of kings, you may be called to hold a civic office and stand against corruption or guide a nation's economy from ruin to health. You may be called to serve in the military and protect freedom or to develop a business that generates revenues to reinvest into solving global problems.

Are you the one who serves behind the scenes? This role is one of the most essential! You may never make an appearance on stage, never be popular on social media, but you're enabling and empowering a team which could not function without the part you play. Bookkeepers, administrators, homemakers, nine-to-fivers - as part of an initiative to bring some element of God's good will into this world, you too are fulfilling your secret calling!

Your secret calling may benefit people through church, business, agriculture, conservation, engineering, fashion, digital media, government, economics, sports, medicine, the arts . . . the list can go on and on.

Nothing worth having is easy. There will be sacrifices. There will be suffering. There will be martyrs. But nothing will be wasted. Nothing will go without reward. Remember, you're the King's ambassador. Your words, your love, your labor represents Him. He declares, "My word . . . shall not return to Me void, but it shall accomplish what I please" (Isa. 55:11 NKJV).

12

CASE STUDY: SEGREGATED TO INFLUENTIAL

"To loose the chains of injustice and untie the cords of the yoke, to set the oppressed free . . . Then your light will break forth like the dawn."

—Isa. 58:6–8

"Speak truth to power, goodness to evil, beauty to crudeness."
—Darrow Miller

Persecution

Hammad skidded into our ministry office. Wrestling his motorcycle helmet off, he blurted, "They attacked Pastor Kashif! They beat him and dragged him to the jail." Almost in tears, Hammad continued, "Right now the mob is demanding they bring him out so they can beat him some more."

CASE STUDY: SEGREGATED TO INFLUENTIAL

Zaheed and I had been discussing the next few months' projects and goals, but with trepidation. These days, all direct proclamation faced increasing opposition. The work of starting communities of faith among those who had no access to the message of Christ suffered constant opposition. New believers were sometimes expelled from their homes and pastors chased out of villages. This latest opposition wasn't unique; in the past week no fewer than three pastors had been beaten up, all in different towns.

Zaheed rose from his desk. His ever-jolly demeanor was weighted. His face was drawn and sad. With a sigh he ran a hand over his nearly gone hairline. Then with a sense of tiredness but duty, he dialed Syed. "Come quick. Kashif is in jail." Moving toward the door with Hammad, he cast back, "Pray. We need favor with the authorities. Again."

I couldn't go with them to the scene. That would exacerbate things because the extremists consider Westerners to be propagators of imperialism. As Zaheed went out, I affirmed, "I'll ask people everywhere to start praying fervently." I tried to sound positive, but the flood of persecution was starting to feel like a whirlpool, draining our strength. We kept thinking it would taper off. But deep down, we wondered if there may be a way to change the entire situation. Was there no key by which to help the people embrace Christ and his communities instead of hating and rejecting them?

Zaheed and Hammad roared away on the motorbikes.

Our office manager Abraham stared blankly at his computer screen. "We're being persecuted," he reasoned, "because the devil is fighting against the gospel work."

"True," I replied, "'All who live godly will suffer persecution.' But these days I'm starting to doubt our traditionalistic conventional interpretation of it. We've credited opposition as being a sign we're on the right track, quoting verses like, 'Blessed are you when you suffer for righteousness.' Or we chalk it up to spiritual warfare, saying, 'The devil is doing it. The devil is fighting against us.'"

"It's what the Bible teaches," said Abraham. "It's inevitable. Persecution will happen, and when it does, we should rejoice."

"Certainly, but what if something is unnecessarily hindering people from seeing Christ in us? What if some of this persecution is unnecessary?"

"Their minds are blinded," said Abraham. "They've chosen to close their hearts. Until they open their hearts, they can't see Christ."

"True. But what if there were a key that would open their hearts, that would show them that he is *good*?"

Defense

Syed could have been a bar bouncer. Like a snow plough, his substantial bulk cleared a path through the raucous protesters. Zaheed and Hammad followed in his wake. Nearly at the steps of the police station, a fierce young man flanked by cronies barred their way. "Who are you?" he shouted. He personified a brown vampire, red snuff dribbling from the corner of his mouth. The mob crowded around, heads swathed in bandannas, sporting black shirts emblazoned with the emblem of their gang. They would like nothing more than a chance to beat up some more Christians.

Zaheed smoothly flashed a lawyer's ID card. "Investigators."

The mob reluctantly moved aside to let them through.

Once inside, they were shown to the office of the chief of police. "The people think you Christians are following a foreign God," he snorted.

"Jesus is just as native to this land as the people themselves," replied Zaheed. "But that's not the point, as you yourself well know. The point is freedom to choose one's faith."

The constable's countenance darkened. He knew the truth.

Zaheed continued, "Those who follow Christ do so of their own free will because they see that he answers prayer. Look at our nation's constitution. Our own law grants people freedom to choose what to believe. So the pastor has done nothing wrong."

"Some of the villagers, the ones shouting outside right now, accused him of disturbing the peace," said the constable.

Zaheed gave him an incredulous look and leaned over, practically into the chief's face. "The pastor was inside his house. Since when is something done inside one's own home 'disturbing the peace'? Sir, you yourself can see it isn't the pastor, but this mob who has 'disturbed the peace.'"

The chief didn't reply. He knew Zaheed was right, but his reputation was at stake. Shuffling papers, he muttered, "I have here a complaint which has been filed against the pastor. On that grounds, he has been incarcerated. You can file for bail. If you wish, you can also file a counter suit."

"Then let us begin." Zaheed helped himself to a chair. "We will file."

From Church to Ekklesia

A few days later, Pastor Kashif was released on bail. A bruise showing through his brown skin and a healing gash above his eye testified of his ordeal, but his heart was merry and his face shone with the joy of Christ.

Zaheed queried, "Do you feel safe to return to your town?"

"I'll return immediately," said Kashif. "The believers need me. They're scared. They need to be encouraged."

"It may be wise," said Zaheed, "to resume church services only after a few weeks, to allow some time for the mob to cool down."

"No," said Kashif. "I will conduct service this Sunday. I will preach the gospel even if it means they kill me. Jesus was persecuted, and I feel honored to suffer for him."

During all of this discussion, my spirit was deeply disturbed. I could see that Zaheed's was as well. At last I ventured to ask, "What if there were a way to show the people that you care about them? To show them that Christians represent hope and life in a broader sense?"

Pastor Kashif became defensive. "I will not compromise the message of the gospel!"

"Of course not," interjected Zaheed. "She doesn't mean that. For example, just think for a moment—what needs are there in the town?"

"Needs? They need Jesus. They need to be saved."

"Of course." Zaheed's voice was patient. "But what physical everyday needs do they have?"

Pastor Kashif bristled. "My job is preaching. The earthly realm is passing away. I stay focused on preaching."

"That's good," I said. "You should most certainly preach and not lose your focus. But for a moment, let's think about your town. Is there poverty?"

"Of course," said Kashif. "Pick any small town in this area, most of the people are poor. But what to do about it? Nothing we can do. Only pray."

"What about the children?" queried Zaheed. "Are there any children who aren't going to school? Or children who are failing their classes because the free local school is not teaching them properly?"

"Oh yes," said Kashif. "There's about twenty children who labor with their parents in the fields. Many more face a dismal future because they're still illiterate even though they're in fifth grade."

"What if someone offered to teach them?"

"They won't come," resolved Kashif. "They don't value education. They think it's a waste of time."

"How can you be sure they don't value education?"

Kashif was silent. "Well, it's just the fact," he muttered.

"The kids who are going to school," I said, "obviously they and their parents value education, or they wouldn't be going."

"What is your wife doing?" inquired Zaheed.

"Hafsah keeps the house. Kids, buffalo, goats, field. She is a wonderful mother and homemaker."

"Does she know how to read and write?"

"A little. She tries to learn more."

"What about your church members? Who among them knows how to read and write?"

"One does. Nazia finished high school. She helps my kids with their school work."

Zaheed and I smiled at each other. We could see the way forward for Kashif to reach and open the hearts of his community.

"Would you consider asking if Nazia and Hafsah would like to start an education center? It could be an after-school program, about two hours a day, so that all the children can learn to read and write."

Multiplied Fruitfulness

Pastor Kashif went home and asked this question of Nazia and of his wife, Hafsah. Both women were elated! They couldn't wait to start an after-school program to help bring education to the whole town.

We Ignite Nations (WIN) provided the financial backing necessary, and within a few weeks the education center opened. At first, some parents hesitated to bring their children to classes, saying, "Those Christians will do nothing but talk about their God." But when they saw the first students coming home and reading the newspaper to their illiterate parents, their perspective changed. Rebellious children became obedient to their parents, and those suffering from depression or anger became happy and peaceful.

After the center had operated for a few months, WIN staff provided hygiene training to Nazia and Hafsah so they in turn could teach it to the children. Soon some of the mothers also began attending the education center and applying what they learned. Families that were once plagued with constant illness became healthier, better nourished, and altogether happier.

From that point on, Pastor Kashif no longer suffered persecution. In fact, the whole town now loved and respected his family and the other believers. The church gatherings occurred without further incident, for the townspeople said, "The Christians are doing good things. Jesus really is good news. The church is a blessing to us and has become a genuine part of the community." Many more people have now become followers of Christ and are being discipled as members of Pastor Kashif's church family.

Because the church became active in solving the community's problems, the kingdom of darkness was pushed back and more of God's kingdom came in. God had been unshrunken. The complete gospel that allows Jesus to be King of all was being both proclaimed and lived.

13

UNLEASHING THE EKKLESIA

"You are the salt of the earth. . . . You are the light of the world."
—Matt. 5:13–14

"The church is the biggest organization on the planet and has the most potential to do good if mobilized."
—Pastor Rick Warren

"Our task . . . is to announce redemption to a world that has discovered its fallenness, to announce healing to a world that has discovered its brokenness, to proclaim love and trust to a world that knows only exploitation, fear and suspicion."
—N. T. Wright

Christ's body, the ekklesia, the church, is the most powerful community on earth. Though having brought great good to the world, deep down we know that something has been missing. We have so much more to give. Though having brought redemption of souls and transformation of lives to some within nearly every tribe tongue and nation, yet we are pained that so many remain without Christ, without hope, broken and tormented. Though having in past eras shown the way to humanity in morality, in freedom, in justice, in charity, today we find ourselves in many cases sidelined, no longer welcomed by a world largely administrated by those outside Christ's kingdom.

Who is to blame for this? Can we say, "The humanists pushed us out" or "Those who oppose the gospel rejected us?" No. Our own partial revelation of Christ has incited the church to intentionally step down from our redemptive inheritance. We ourselves have chosen to muzzle our prophetic voice.

What has been missing? Nothing other than our secret calling! Now is the time to arise! At any moment the slumbering princess can awake to her full purpose! The church can, by the power and the mercy of Christ, don her crown and re-engage as the priceless, prized, and also persecuted steward of the earth, the King's healer bringing life and wholeness both spiritually and physically.

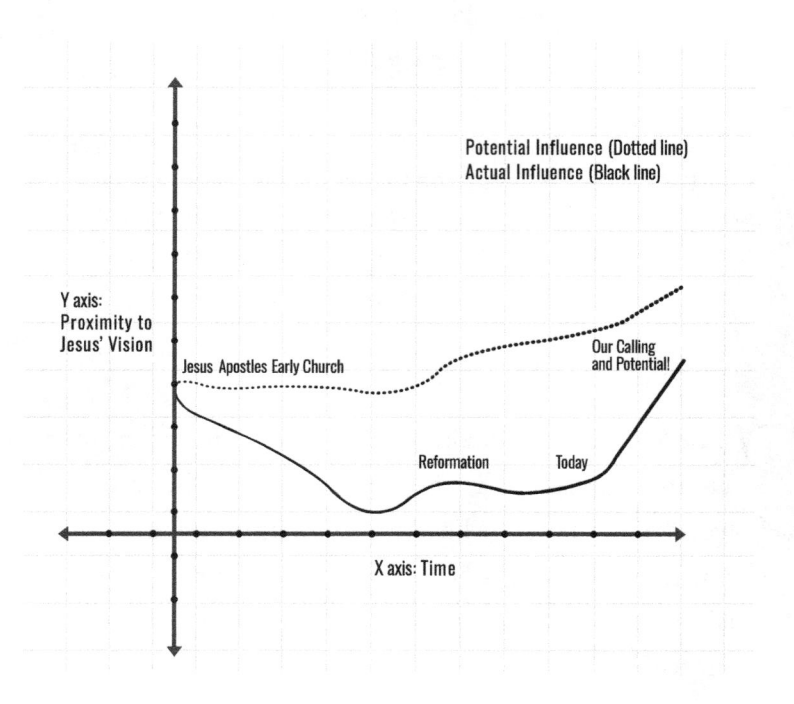

In the above illustration, the *dotted* trajectory is that which the church could have fulfilled throughout history had we apprehended the fullness of our inheritance, patterning our lives after Jesus' example and our assemblies after his full redemptive purpose. The *solid* trajectory is our actual proximity to Jesus' vision, the degree to which we've experienced and unleashed into the world his highest purpose.

However, here's the good news: Notice that the trajectories become thicker as they progress through time. The church is incredibly strong today! Were a significant percentage of believers and kingdom communities in this latter hour to step into God's highest purpose, the trajectory could skyrocket. A tsunami of healing can be released—redemption of souls and healing of a wounded world. Lostness, poverty, addiction, oppression, and crime will be driven back through the healing, life-giving, whole-person, and all-life-redeeming goodness of the good King's ekklesia.

The first step in allowing Jesus to transition our lives, our assemblies called churches, and all kingdom communities toward his vision of ekklesia, is no longer to be satisfied to keep the world out. We will go out to the world. We will no longer be satisfied with caring for spiritual children. Now the children will be trained and will grow into adults. We will no longer see ourselves as a lunar landing pod awaiting ejection to heaven. Instead, we will repossess territory stolen by the pandemic (Josh. 1:3), confident in our commission both "to seek and to save the lost" (Luke 19:10) and "seek the peace and prosperity of the city" (Jer. 29:7).

> The church will no longer be seen by some as irrelevant but as transformational, not so much as opposers of ungodly culture, but as creators and builders of righteous culture.

> Evacuation will happen in the Lord's time. In the meantime, we will be focused on occupation.

Our traditional view of "church" as a gathered community is by no means wrong, but it is incomplete. It must be completed, liberated, and empowered by the kingdom view:

Traditional View	Kingdom View
Religious service	God's legislative assembly
Hospital	Laboratory
Nursing home	Incubator
Fortress—safety from evil	Battalion—conquest of evil
Fellowship	Harvest
Family	Rescue squad, special forces

How can the organized church be unshrunk? How can a traditional church community allow Jesus to build His ekklesia? How can we transition from the vicious circle of irrelevancy into being a healer of the sin pandemic and of its spin-off diseases that plague our world?

The biblical paradigms offered in the preceding pages have removed the shrink wrap from God. You've been equipped with ancient keys by which to see a more complete picture of Jesus, human beings, and the church. You've experienced case studies that provide real-life examples.

Now it's time for further practical training, specific areas of transition by which your individual life generally and kingdom communities specifically can become ambassadors carrying God's highest purpose into our wounded world.

From Service to Shalom

Why is church planting so important? The gates of Hades represent entry points and establishments of demonic governance, the enemy's kingdom of death. God's kingdom of life also has entry points and establishments. Wherever a new ekklesia—a community of faith—is established, a "gate" of *life* is opened! An entry point for God's good reign is set in the midst of the town or region.

But our perception of "church planting" is too small for King Jesus, who came to "plant" not a limited institution but his unlimited kingdom!

Evangelism invites individuals to faith and repentance, enjoining them to come "out of darkness into his wonderful light" (1 Pet. 2:9). But church planting establishes the community, the leadership, and the environment wherein discipleship, baptism, and teaching occur. Church planting is the essential wheel revolving around Christ the hub. It is the establishment of a sustainable, persistent portal of light illuminating a region that formerly was "walking in darkness" (Isa. 9:2; Matt. 4:16).

In a similar but somewhat different way, a kingdom business or other community that enthrones Christ and lives worthy of his kingship brings his kingdom into the physical dimensions and invites his good rule into the community, the city, and the culture. Hearts that were otherwise closed are opened, bringing them closer to becoming citizens themselves.

Jesus and then the apostles demonstrated and proclaimed Jesus the whole-life Deliverer. Thus, "the word of God spread. The number of disciples . . . increased rapidly" (Acts 6:7). Three chapters later, "The churches . . . were multiplied" (Acts 9:31 NKJV). What increased? The Word of God, the disciples, and the communities of disciples.

What constitutes a community of disciples, a "church"?

Let us remember that the actual term translated "church" throughout the New Testament is ekklesia—the legislative community of the good reign of the good King reunited with his beloved creation. Not a religious service. Certainly not a building or a denomination.

New Testament ekklesia assemblies were people-centric, not program-centric, and usually involved something for everyone to enjoy: food, drink, and interactive relationship!

Organized church assemblies are essential. The command to "not [forsake] the assembling of ourselves together" indicates a structured community that occurs on a regular basis and includes practices essential and core to healthy discipleship: learning the Word of God, corporate prayer and worship, partaking of the Lord's supper, and baptism of new believers (Hebrew 10:25 NKJV).

However, we must stop limiting church planting to what we view as, and make into, religious institutions. Jesus is King of all. King Jesus' ekklesia is intended to possess the gates. That means the church is to influence the whole city, society, and nation. That means his life is to be established in the very places where the gates of death, the government of the pandemic, currently executes its ruinous rule.

> God's highest purpose will be fulfilled when we allow him to expand us from only conducting services to conducting his shalom into all of life.

Jesus said, "Where two or three gather in my name, there am I with them" (Matt. 18:20). Believers can assemble ekklesia anywhere—in a coffee shop, during lunch at the workplace, in a pub, or while hiking up a mountain. An ekklesia assembly may be as small as a single family or as big as a megachurch or as unconventional as a kingdom business. When that community proceeds to live as true disciples of Christ demonstrating his goodness, a bulwark is erected against the destructive intent of the enemy. The demonic archon of the kingdom of darkness, the evil "prince" of the region, has some competition and can no longer freely bring pandemics upon the people (Dan. 10:13). From this ekklesia community, Christ's reconciliation can now radiate.

There's a reason Jesus used yeast and salt to illustrate his vision for his community (Matt. 13:33; 5:13). In his day, both were among the most common ingredients found in a kitchen. Like yeast when kneaded into dough, Christ's ekklesia is to penetrate all things as representatives of Christ. If the yeast is not mixed well, the bread will rise unevenly. Part will be hard and heavy; another part will be ballooned by air bubbles. When all aspects of God's goodness are mixed into all aspects of society, then an exponential transformation will occur, just like the raw, dull lump of dough becomes a beautiful golden brown loaf.

This is a thing that has almost never been done throughout history, for we have never truly understood our secret calling and God's highest purpose, nor have we perceived the biblical keys to actuate it.

Have you ever chowed down on some yummy-looking food only for the first bite to reveal that the cook forgot the salt? Scrambled eggs especially are a bland mass of mush without salt! Though invisible once absorbed into the food, you know it is there because it accentuates flavor. As salt makes good better, so remember, you're made in the Creator's image to "tend"—to create, to cultivate, to further develop God's stuff.

> Churches and kingdom communities are to be entry points through which the kingdom of life injects healing and good into all of society.

Salt also preserves food from spoilage, and when applied to a wound, the patient feels momentary pain but the infection that would have led to amputation or death is driven out. Likewise, we are to "keep guard" (Gen. 2:15), preserving what is good and purifying what is contaminated. The powers of darkness will oppose, but they will not prevail.

So in our all-important "church planting," remember that Jesus isn't building institutions but a citizenship that influences everything around it. Not a service, but a community that demonstrates and radiates shalom. And seeing this, "the light [that] shines in the darkness" will be comprehended (John 1:5). More darkened hearts will see and repent and turn to the light.

From Irrelevant to Essential

The irrelevance of the organized church and of believers individually is fueled first of all by our failure to live as true disciples. This is why Jesus so vehemently warned against religious hypocrisy (Matt. 23). If his kingdom people engage in the same evil as those still in the kingdom of death, neither should we complain if we are sidelined.

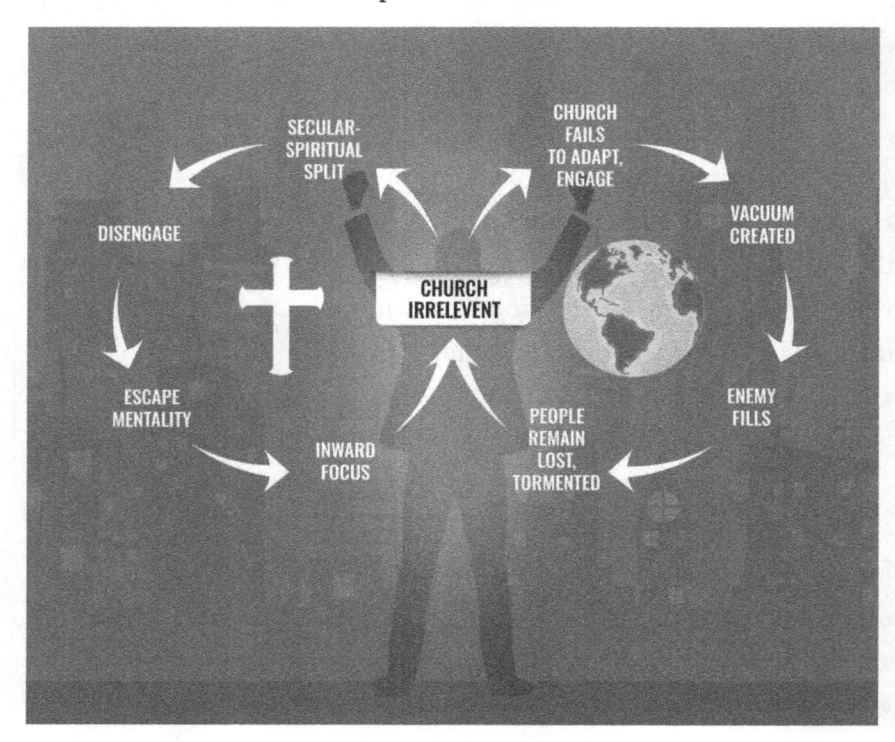

The second driver of our irrelevance is our disconnect with life. Jesus' vision is discipleship of people with his end goal being discipleship of nations. But we have failed to see this bigger vision and have diminished the gospel, making it less great than Jesus intended. Because of this, "the vast bulk of the Western world no longer believes in the Bible and no longer follows our faith—partly because believers in general have not been at the forefront of efforts to defeat evil."[1]

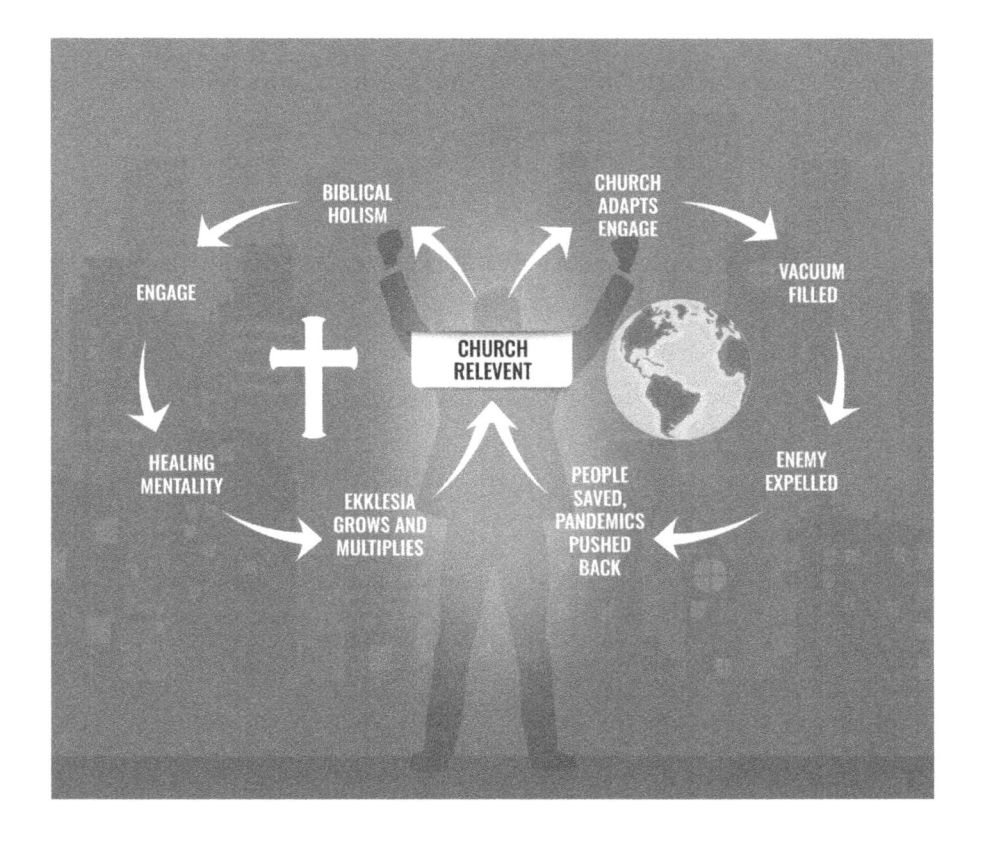

When we dare to represent the whole, unshrunken gospel of God's kingdom, then the church becomes relevant without compromise. We steward our "promised land" through bringing Christ's salvation spiritually and practically into business, media, government, the arts, engineering, education, medicine, sports, and all of life. When this happens, the community will say, "The churches are essential services. Without them, society goes astray, crime increases, homicides and suicides increase. We fear what would happen to our city if the church were not here and active! No matter what, we can't close the churches."

Mega and Micro

Participation in ancient Israel's ekklesia assembly was both a privilege and injunction that came with citizenship in the kingdom. Likewise, the physical assembly of believers is a commandment and a nonnegotiable (Heb. 10:25).

Brick and mortar spaces—be they homes, storefronts, steepled chapels, vast megachurch complexes, businesses, seminaries, ministries, missions, schools, and hospitals—all play an essential role in Christ's ekklesia agenda in this season.

In these end times, the buildings will now transition. They will not be an end in themselves nor the focal point. They will be tools wielded by anointed believers, pastors, entrepreneurs, apostolic leaders, and prophetic ministers.

> The point is not to fill the building but to make disciples of everything outside the building.

The buildings will become launch pads for mission, for the deliverance of the people who are not in the building. They will be training grounds, equipping centers, places where people find real healing and then go forth to heal others and to bring his healing into every sector of life. They will be incubators of life, hubs of enrichment where the soul-saving, uncompromising good news of the kingdom is carried into hearts through the laid-down lives of true disciple ambassadors who incarnate the King's goodness.

From Compromise to Courage

As in the Book of Revelation the dragon waits to consume the newly birthed child (Rev. 12:4), so today the powers of darkness stand at the door, seeking opportunity to undermine the strength of Christ's community. At this very moment many are losing their saltiness. Thinking they are being relevant, seeker-friendly, or loving, some are compromising timeless biblical truths of God's Word. Thinking they promote freedom, they align instead with the government of death that enslaves. Those who were intended to steward and guard the earth and align it with a holy and good Father God are instead allowing themselves to be realigned to the pattern of the pandemic. How can we bring healing when we bow to the lie that broken is actually another form of normal?

If those entrusted to administer the balm of Gilead agree to the pandemic's cruel diagnosis that the wounded are just made that way and don't need healing, then we have denied Christ's broken body, which was wounded for our healing. If we who hold the keys of life cast off society as the domain of Satan, we have also cast our divinely entrusted keys of the kingdom into the devil's altar of compromise. We have failed to truly *love*, for true love says, "You might have given up on yourself, but I won't give up on you, because you are precious and valuable."

Because of Jesus' victory, today we must only choose whose kingdom to belong to and which kingdom to promote. But deception is at an all-time high. Carefully discern the difference between kingdoms. Will the church wake up in time and run from Korah to Moses (Num. 16)? Or will we bow to the sin pandemic, to Satan who "masquerades as an angel of light" (2 Cor. 11:14)? Will we stand with the King of all who has "the words of eternal life" (John 6:68)? "Woe to those who call evil

> Jesus didn't contend for a mere earthly kingdom; he defeated the kingdom of death that enslaves all earthly kingdoms.

good and good evil, who put darkness for light and light for darkness" (Isa. 5:20). Therefore, "choose for yourselves this day whom you will serve" (Josh. 24:15).

Adam and Eve were entrusted to keep guard and to subdue that which was not in alignment with God's goodness. So also we today are entrusted to stand stalwart, with compassion and mercy, with gentle firmness, with courage and patience. We should be "seen as lights in the world, holding forth the word of life," banners, forward-moving billboards both showing the way and leading the way to the good King's life-giving ways, which unleash healing and wholeness in all dimensions for all people (Phil. 2:15–16 ASV; Isa. 11:12).

From Ignored to Opposed

"Everyone who wants to live a godly life in Christ Jesus will be persecuted" (2 Tim. 3:12). Living out your secret calling will include opposition, because frightened bears fight and cornered skunks spray!

> When we incarnate whole-life salvation so that both spiritual and material poverty are dispelled and his goodness is seen and demonstrated, then the spiritual powers of darkness tremble.

The spiritual archons of the pandemic are terrified when the King's appointed stewards of earth become true disciples and, by the power of his Spirit live lives that reflect his goodness. Those dark powers become even more frightened when those disciples take his healing outward into society. When the King's ekklesia begins to meet "in the gates" and not only in the religious places—when we acknowledge that suicide and crime are trespassers and that the businesses, the streets, the families, and the government all belong to the good King who authors life and peace—then the Gates of Hades are shaken.

When we put action to this realization and begin to pray for our cities, when we take our praise and worship out into the public places, when we serve "the least of these" in a way that sustainably solves problems in his name, the gates of death are invaded by heaven's life, love and liberty.

Therefore, don't be caught off guard. You are called to be a soldier and an athlete (2 Tim. 2:3.; 1 Cor. 9:24). Both require discipline, courage, and a willingness to suffer if and when necessary in order to persevere in the cause. Though freed from the dichotomy that devalues earthly things, remember that prestige and wealth make good servants but miserable masters (1 Tim. 6:10). The spiritual guides and aligns and stewards the physical. Arm yourself with the mind of Christ, "who, being in very nature God, did not consider equality with God something to be used to his own advantage; rather, he made himself nothing by taking the very nature of a servant" (Phil. 2:6–7).

Our job in this life is to incarnate Christ as his body, living and active in the world, demonstrating his good rule—his kingdom—even as he did. But this world has been ravaged by the pandemic of death for millennia. Should we expect the principalities to simply hand over the reins? No. They will oppose. They will resist. Our job is neither to bow to their violent or unrighteous methods nor to back down and become silent. Stand firm and press on. This season is training for reigning. "Let's not become discouraged in doing good, for in due time we will reap, if we do not become weary" (Gal. 6:9 NASB).

From Programs to Presence and Power

It is very important that church communities offer biblically sound teaching, engaging worship experiences and programs that minister to the people. But all this must be infused with the presence and power of the living Lord Jesus. The first step in healing the land is for God's people to "humble themselves . . . and turn from their wicked ways" (2 Chron. 7:14). When people repent and forgive, the King of Righteousness draws near and we see his glory. To be a conduit of his power we must offer ourselves as a vessel of his presence.

Worship is the next step. Don't be satisfied with mere cerebral song singing. True worship is the connection of our spirit to his. Thereby, we enter the throne room where we see his glory and cry, "Woe is me" (Isa. 6:5). There he touches us with his cleansing, healing fire and sets us upon our feet where we then declare in joy and expectation, "Here am I. Send me!" (Isa. 6:8).

Hosting the King's presence also means our assemblies fulfill biblical decency and orderliness while not quenching the Holy Spirit (1 Cor. 14:40; 1 Thess. 5:19). How to "test the spirits, whether they are of God" (1 John 4:1)? Ask, "Is Jesus being lifted up?" and "Are people being drawn to Him? Are lives being changed?" If so, then best not to criticize.

Remember, the purpose of the infilling of the Spirit is "power" so that we may "be [his] witnesses" (Acts 1:8). God's not dead! Jesus is *alive*! He is just as alive today as he was when he walked on the water, cast out demons, and healed incurable diseases. But how will he show himself alive today if not through his ambassadors, his citizen generals, his ekklesia legislative community?

> Embark on a journey to discover what it means to join the King in his court, to be filled and refilled with his Spirit . . . But don't keep the fullness in!

Arising from that place of worship and praise, he wants to ignite strategic prayer initiatives that focus not on personal needs but outward, on the people beyond the fold, and the life going on around us.

A theology that relegates God's miraculous and supernatural works to bygone eras is just one more expression of a partial, divided, and paganized reduction. It constitutes not letting God be King of all because it declares him able to heal the soul but not able or willing to influence the physical dimension by healing bodies. Remember, you're his steward, keeping guard of the world and the people he loves. The one who spoke and life came into being wants to speak through you. The same Holy Spirit who anointed the earliest disciples to heal and cast out demons empowers you (Mark 16:17–18, Acts 1:8, 1 Cor. 12:7–10). He wants your lips, anointed by his Spirit, in alignment with Scripture and subjection to his will, to declare deliverance and healing in the authority of Jesus to whom "all authority in heaven and earth" has been delegated. Let us go about our lives expecting a living God to show himself mighty to heal and deliver through us. As we do so, his whole, multiplied glory will be released!

From Charity to Love

The word *charity* at one time was synonymous with love. However, today charity means "giving of money or other help to those in need."[2]

Apart from catastrophic disaster situations such as fire, flood, and war, the healing kingdom response to human need should not be mere charity. Charity is *not* love, because handouts do not heal. In the long run, giving free stuff disempowers and enslaves the very people our good intentions had intended to help. To the extent that we endeavor to be healers of earth's pandemic of poverty, we must not yield to the emotional strokes we get by feeding and clothing people who appear helpless. The enemy wants us to see them as helpless, because to the extent we continue to feed their dependency, they will become less and less able to climb out of the pit. "People need trade, not aid. They don't need a hand out, they need a hand up."

Manna was God's welfare system, his "unemployment compensation" and "food stamps." But it was Plan B, because his Plan A had been to take them straight into the promised land, where they would prosper based on their own labor. When he at last was able to execute his "job placement plan" and distribute to them his "microfinance startup capital," he didn't just give it to them. They had to fight! They had to exert effort—work—to possess the land on which they would from then on become self-sustaining. God's welfare system was not perpetual. It ended as soon as the people had been empowered to generate their own sustenance.

> Charity is cruel when not associated with genuine empowerment into sustainable thriving.

Poverty is just one more manifestation of the sin pandemic. As Christ's ekklesia stewards and guardians of Earth, in every circumstance of need we must ask, "How can I empower this person so that they have both the desire and the ability to overcome poverty?" Now you are operating as a healer, an ambassador of the King who sets people free from slavery.

Mini Case Study: Hens Versus Hunger

Like a giant serpentine, a strip of pavement barely wide enough for two vehicles to pass, twisted its way up the steep slope. Gabor, WIN's native leader of this nation, skillfully maneuvered the SUV around hairpin turns. The sheer abyss beyond the road's shoulderless edge seemed only a few feet from the wheels. Below and behind lay the nation's capital city. Our destination was a rural area where we would encourage native believers in their homes. I would soon experience the "real" country outside the tourist zone's prosperous facade.

Gabor slowed the vehicle and pointed across the valley. "Over there is some vacant land. Our nation's leaders want someone to develop it."

In the distance where he was pointing rose a steep mountain slope without any hint of civilization, not even a road.

"Whether there or somewhere else," continued Gabor, "someday we'd like to start a project that will provide a service to the community, generate income, and also enable us to provide Bible training to new leaders."

Gabor almost never uses the word "I." He is always thinking "team" and endeavoring to build-up others. Native to a land in which churches are not permitted to exist openly, and where gatherings of Christians must either be very small or inconspicuous, Gabor is a dynamic youth leader. Each year he gets around four hundred young people to travel across the border into a nearby country where he leads them in worship, Bible study, and committing their lives to serve Christ and respect their country and culture.

When I first met him, he was using his own resources to transport Bibles all over his nation, encouraging believers in remote places who have little contact with the outside world. Gabor follows in the footsteps of his father who despite persecution, established thirteen indigenous churches.

I returned home and a few months later, the Covid pandemic struck. WIN's courageous native leaders provided food relief to suffering families in several nations where we work. In one nation when the hospitals were so full that those needing oxygen couldn't get it, we provided portable oxygen machines that our leaders carried around on their motorbikes, saving lives. When we learned that seventy-five pastors' wives in our network knew how to sew but had no sewing machine, we provided the machines along with training in how to make and sell urgently needed but simple products. These women received dignity as well as the ability to ensure their children never go hungry.

As time went on, I realized I had not heard from Gabor. Finally, I reached out to him and asked, "How are things in your nation? Like others, are you under lockdown and struggling for food to survive?"

Gabor replied, "Yes, we are totally locked down and suffering greatly." Then, anticipating that I was about to offer money for food, he added, "but don't send us any charity!"

His words took me by surprise, and I immediately sensed that something of God's kingdom was about to happen. "Is there anything we can do to help?" I asked.

"We want to start some businesses," said Gabor. "Three small businesses to help people feed their families."

For those three microbusiness his request was fifteen hundred dollars. WIN immediately released the funds and within two months received a very nice report. They had started three businesses: a small textile shop producing and selling face masks and simple clothing items, a bakery producing biscuits and crackers, and an organic vegetable farm supplying nutritious food that had become scarce due to the lockdown.

Gabor and his team had proven themselves with these small projects, so I inquired, "What do you want to do next?"

Then he told me something that left me speechless:

"Our nation has the highest per capita meat consumption in the entire continent. Our people love to eat meat. It is an important food source for us. However, the religious beliefs of the majority of our people here forbid them from taking a life. For them, it's morally wrong to kill an animal even for food. But as long as the meat is processed by someone else, our people feel OK to eat it."

"So," I puzzled, "How do they get meat?"

"They import it," said Gabor. "Up to 80% of many of our meats are shipped in from abroad."

"Fascinating," I said. "So what's the problem?"

"Because of the Covid pandemic, our borders are closed," replied Gabor. "We cannot receive anything imported, and are now forced to survive on whatever our own nation produces. Because there is so little local meat production, our people are going without meat."

I about jumped out of my chair! "Wow, what an opportune moment to provide a solution," I exclaimed. "What do you propose to do?"

"Remember that land I pointed out?" asked Gabor. "We want to start a poultry and pork farm."

Gabor and I prayed together about the initiative and I invited him to submit a proposal. Within a short time, he had prepared a very detailed business plan.

Through the sacrificial contribution of his local friends and believers, Gabor raised almost a quarter of the needed funding, and WIN provided the balance.

Then began the daunting task of building a road up the mountain! Gabor admits that it was a bigger job than he had expected but he didn't lose heart, and poured all of his effort as well as wisdom into the project. Once the bulldozer had cut a rough road up to the proposed construction site the next step was to flatten out large areas of the mountain. Finally construction began on the sheds to house the chickens. Meanwhile Gabor received training in poultry farm management.

Back in the US we waited prayerfully and looked forward to every update. Gabor is an excellent communicator and regularly shared photos of the construction progress.

After about six months the facility was ready and the first batch of chicks arrived. The chicks grew rapidly and within three months were ready for market, while a second batch had already been started.

Honoring the local culture and religious beliefs, Gabor's team of Christian workers processed the chickens so that customers did not have to violate their consciences.

Within the first six months of operation the farm produced an astounding nine tons of meat! The government was the primary customer. Trucks came out to the farm and bought 500 chickens at a time to feed the people of the city.

In its first year of operation the farm turned a healthy profit and Gabor reinvested it into expanding the operations, adding layer hens and pigs.

Last year Gabor married a lovely young lady from a more urbanized area who had no farm experience. She has been a real trooper, living out there on the farm, managing it while he is away and even helping wash chicken poop off of seven thousand eggs a day!

In addition to solving the meat deficit for the capital city, the farm is providing jobs to people who otherwise would be in poverty, and the farm's profits are being reinvested into setting up more families with their own micro businesses, and providing Bible training to new believers.

Only a year and a half after its launch, the farm had made such an impact that the government declared it a model of excellence, an example to the nation. A reporter was sent out to interview Gabor and the farm was praised on the national media.

Because this project is developed through local believers who are living their faith boldly and unashamedly, a nation is seeing that Christ and his people provide solutions and bring good things into society. An element of the kingdom of darkness—hunger and lack—is being sustainably solved and an element of the kingdom of light—provision and sufficiency—is being demonstrated.

This is just one example of what can happen when God is not limited to just the spiritual or the unseen realm. When his goodness is allowed to flow through us into all sectors of life, whole sectors of society can be healed and the heart of a nation can be changed!

Of all the ancient keys so far, one last series of keys remains to be revealed. This secret arkenstone crowns them all and multiplies the magnificent potential of your secret calling.

14

THE KEY TO EXPONENTIAL GOOD

"All authority in heaven and on earth has been given to me. Therefore go and make disciples of all nations."

Matt. 28:18-19

"And I, when I am lifted up from the earth, will draw all people to myself."

—John 12:32

"Christ the Mediator is setting up a kingdom in the world, bring the nations to be his subjects; setting up a school, bring the nations to be his scholars; raising an army for the carrying on of the war against the (spiritual) powers of darkness, enlist the nations of the earth under his banner."

— Matthew Henry

King Jesus spent three years demonstrating that God's kingdom heals and redeems all sectors of life, both the temporal now and the eternal forever. Through his death and resurrection he destroyed the power of the sin pandemic, the devil's kingdom of death. He inaugurated his legislative community and declared the keys—the authority of the kingdom of life—handed over to his citizen officers.

Then just before ascending to take his place enthroned on the right hand of the Father, Jesus declared, "All authority in heaven and on earth has been given to me" (Matt. 28:18).

Notice that Jesus has *all* authority in *both* heaven and earth and has conveyed it to his ekklesia citizens. Heaven is the originator and empowerer of his will on earth. Earth is to reflect and celebrate heaven. Heaven and earth were not intended to be divided into two opposing and mutually hostile zones. They were to form a closed circuit resulting in glorious, supernatural multiplication of God's redemption and deliverance from darkness.

What does this mean? Nothing less than that what Jesus uttered next - what we call the Great Commission—is also meant to affect not only the eternal but also the earthly—and therein lies a great secret, the ancient key to exponential healing of souls and also society!

The GREAT Great Commission

"Therefore go and make disciples of all nations" (Matt. 28:19). This grand deputation summarizes God's highest purpose and our secret calling. However we have tragically misunderstood and diminished it. The powers of darkness so dread that the King's citizen officers would understand and carry out his full intention contained in this passage, that they have deceived us into thinking it applies only or primarily to those few with a peculiar "missionary" calling who pack their suitcases and venture off to some remote corner of the biosphere. In truth, the

Great Commission encapsulates and mobilizes the entire *missio dei*, the whole purpose of God in healing and restoring human beings and creation into life, love and liberty.

"All nations"—*pante ethnos*—means "all ethnicities" or "all people groups." One or more individuals from "every nation, tribe, people and language" must become a citizen of God's kingdom through faith in Jesus (Rev. 7:9). Initiatives to make Christ's love and salvation available to every "unreached" tribe and every human soul are essential. Our Father God does not want "anyone to perish, but everyone to come to repentance" (2 Pet. 3:9).

But the world's reception of God's love gift has been hindered by our having failed to see the whole picture.

Whenever the word *ethnos* occurs in the New Testament it refers not only to individuals and ethnicities but to geopolitical groups—nations. God has always dealt with territories, cities, and nations: Eden, Babel, Ur, Egypt, the promised land, Jerusalem, Babylon. In the New Testament, Jesus wept over Jerusalem and prophesied the future of nations.

In Mark's rendering of the Great Commission, Jesus commands us to "go into all the world" (Mark 16:15). The Greek *kosmos* is beyond geography. It means the entirety of the world—people in their cities, their unique cultures, their religions, and their geopolitical groupings. Taken at face value, the passage indicates the good news of the kingdom is to permeate every manifestation of each grouping of humanity. God's good kingdom is to be represented and manifested not only in individual lives. Like salt, light, and leaven, those individual lives are to manifest and incarnate his goodness, truth, and beauty in every demography, geography, and ideology.

So if we dare to interpret this literally, we would agree that "nations" means more people than just those who frequent a Bible study or outreach event. And it means more than just individual human hearts. It means communities, civilizations, and *nations*!

Why would Jesus have any lower vision, since he is *King* and kings own *everything*? Why would he have any smaller agenda, since he authorized his people to "possess the gate of their enemies" (Gen. 22:17 NASB)? This does not imply top-down dominionism. It means subduing spiritual wickedness, and also being servant leaders protecting the Earth garden and all its people, being salt and light, demonstrating and teaching the good King's kingdom so that all may experience shalom.

But there's more!

Discipleship Unleashed

Most believers agree that restoration of relationship, emancipation from the kingdom of darkness, and naturalization into the kingdom of light all happen by faith and not by "works," i.e., not by our own righteousness or good deeds (Eph. 2:8–9). However, faith without the attestation of a righteous lifestyle and good deeds is "dead." "I will show you my faith by my deeds" (James 2:17–18).

We have been missing the secret key that lies within this truth. To the degree that we endeavor to guide people to the kingdom of life without also demonstrating it in a tangible way, they are likely to say, "Where are the works that prove your faith is real and your God is alive?" To the degree that we allow our proclamation of faith to be undergirded and attested by demonstration in the felt needs of those around us, they will say, "Now I can see that your faith is powerful. I want what you have. Tell me more."

> If we limit the gospel to the intangible and otherworldly, if we limit it to "forgiveness of sin," we will always view the tangible and this-worldly as a threat and our audience will be limited to those few who already sense a need for things of a spiritual nature.

Most human beings are like second graders who know how to add but would be baffled by algebra. We understand things like the need for bodily healing, economic sufficiency, and human rights. But we may not perceive a need for spiritual salvation or believe that Jesus is the 'formula" for it. Neither do we see how the tangible plus the spiritual "adds up" to the answer for which everyone longs—shalom both here and in the hereafter.

For this very reason Jesus' miracles engaged people in their immediate felt needs. By healing, provision, justice, and mercy Jesus demonstrated the kingdom principles and the triumph of God's life over the evil one's death pandemic. He fired the synapse where God's kingdom touches earth. All the while, he constantly proclaimed the Kingdom, pointing them to the source of the goodness they were witnessing.

The physical manifestation of God's kingdom, the physical healing of the consequences of the sin pandemic, brought people to a place where they could see that they also needed to be healed spiritually, reunited with Father God.

When we both demonstrate and proclaim the kingdom as Jesus himself modeled, people are drawn to us because we are meeting them where they are, in the midst of their real-world needs and dreams.

A well-known diagram shows the cross of Christ forming the bridge for people to emigrate from death to life. But what that diagram omits is the fact that there's a problem! As I have illustrated above, most people are not paying attention and are not crossing over. They do not realize that Jesus is their answer. Instead, they are facing the other way, about to commit suicide or otherwise fall into the abyss of death and destruction.

Today the vast majority of people are convinced that "Christians" or "the church" is irrelevant, corrupt, outdated. But the same people are broken and tormented by drugs and addictions, phobias, and depression. Or they carry on with life thinking they are happy but never seeing their need for Christ. How will they see and choose to turn to the light?

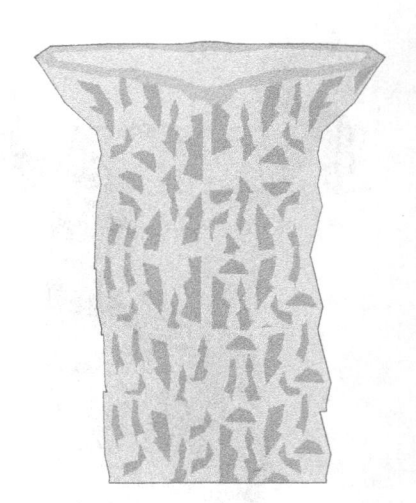

The above modification illustrates the social gospel, the opposite extreme which abandons the core message of salvation and hurls itself primarily into trying to change human society. It forgets that the keys of the kingdom are the only thing powerful enough to heal earth's pandemic and human brokenness. When spiritual salvation—the transfer of human souls from the kingdom of darkness to the kingdom of light—is sidelined, we sell our birthright for a bowl of porridge and exchange our royal gold for hay and stubble.

How will people be aided to see Christ's love and power? Indeed, "in him [Jesus] was life, and the life was the light of mankind" and "the light shines in the darkness," but "the darkness did not grasp it" (John 1:4, 5). How will "The people walking in darkness" see his light? How will the dark world around us see that his Kingdom is life and peace and the solution to every human problem? These final keys are found in two secret concepts; demonstration, and pre-discipleship.

Demonstration

Most human beings are like second graders who know how to add but would be baffled by algebra. We understand things like the need for bodily healing, economic sufficiency, and human rights. But we may not perceive a need for spiritual salvation or believe that Jesus is the 'formula" for it. Neither do we see how the tangible plus the spiritual "adds up" to the answer for which everyone longs—shalom both here and in the hereafter.

For this very reason Jesus' miracles engaged people in their immediate felt needs. By healing, provision, justice, and mercy Jesus demonstrated the kingdom principles and the triumph of God's life over the evil one's death pandemic. He fired the synapse where God's kingdom touches earth. All the while, he constantly proclaimed the kingdom, pointing them to the source of the goodness they were witnessing.

The physical manifestation of God's kingdom, the physical healing of the consequences of the sin pandemic, brought people to a place where they could see that they also needed to be healed spiritually, reunited with Father God.

When we both demonstrate and proclaim the kingdom as Jesus himself modeled, people are drawn to us because we are meeting them where they are, in the midst of their real-world needs and dreams.

Pre-Discipleship

Discipleship of believers is essential, but what about discipleship of pre-believers? Jesus "discipled" thousands—even his own inner circle—before they ever confessed him as Lord. In today's language, we might have called them "seekers." He didn't say, "Believe in me and confess me, and then we can start Bible school." He demonstrated while he proclaimed, proclaimed while he demonstrated. Far from being in opposition to one another, the two were explosively complementary.

Pre-salvation discipleship is necessary for people like Zacchaeus who don't come to a "service" but watch from a safe distance, like Peter who carry on their their business unaware of their need for Christ, and like Saul who opposed Christ and inadvertently promoted the works of darkness. All these are "pre-discipleship" candidates who would not likely turn to the kingdom of light without an intentional demonstration of it.

People are drawn to the kingdom because they see through our lives the power of Christ and a higher way. This concept is simply illustrated by a further revision of the cross-and-chasm diagram:

The first thing you might notice here is, thankfully, the cross is back in its rightful position, creating the one-and-only bridge by which human beings can cross from death to life. Secondly, our precious soul who was about to leap or fall from the cliff into destruction, and who was completely unaware of, resistant to, or uninterested in the cross, has stood up, turned toward it, and is stepping into the light!

What has incited this radical turning toward the hope and healing offered by Christ? The answer is found in the rays emanating outward and the believer who has engaged with the people and their environment. Believers are no longer just standing over there in the light calling "Come to Jesus!" And no, this is not intended to illustrate a mission trip! The believer is not making a "bombing raid" to extract this soul but rather has genuinely engaged, with the interest not only of rescuing one soul but of demonstrating God's kingdom and driving back darkness. The believer is recognizing that the world around us, the soup we live in—i.e., life—*matters*. The atmosphere around the other person is no longer ignored or deemed to be impenetrable or hopeless. The possibility of illuminating the darkness is acknowledged and acted upon.

God's will of peace, provision, and purpose comes to earth, while also his spiritual salvation is received.

But this still falls short of what God has in store for us! Here comes the final key and the crowning secret!

Magnetic Multiplication

Recall the below diagram which was shared earlier and its message—that the demonstration of God's goodness is powerful to bring light, hope and healing into all sectors of life. Light influences the darkness, not the other way around. This is the "defragmented Gospel," the full gospel of the kingdom. Those who live this out are discipling their world, being witnesses not only in word but also in deed, "demonstrational witnesses."

> When citizens of the kingdom engage in demonstration and pre-salvation discipleship as Jesus did, people who would not have perceived that God exists, or who would have continued in a pattern of selfdestruction, instead see that God is good.

Now let me share the final and capstone ancient key, made available to us by understanding the preceding keys:

Where life and deeds demonstrate God's goodness in the natural arena of felt needs, and where simultaneously unashamed proclamation is made of Christ's saving and redeeming atonement, the miraculous happens: what may have been perceived as purely physical is transformed into something holy. Now there is no more mere "social work." Nothing is "secular." Every action that reflects God's good will of shalom becomes a demonstration of his good kingdom on earth. Every word spoken of Christ's salvation is authenticated by validating deeds. This results in an ever-expanding ripple effect of outward-flowing healing, salvation, and transformation.

But that's not all! Remember the frustration and sense of "Isn't there more?" under which so many today languish? Here is the lack we're sensing:

We are supposed to be MAGNETS!

This is illustrated in the diagram below:

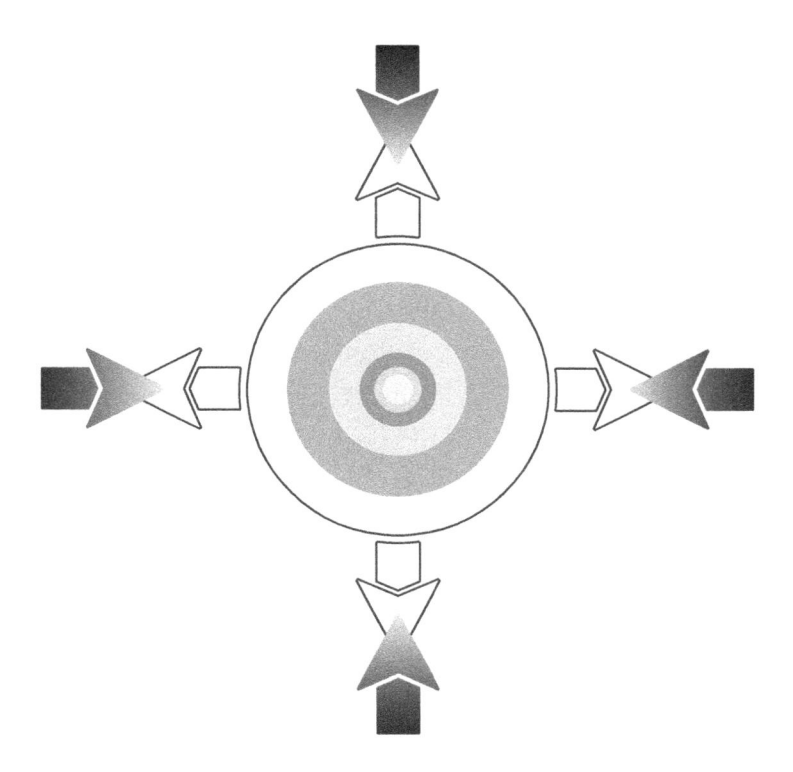

The circular areas represent the world we live in - life in all its facets both spiritual and physical. The white circles represent God's kingdom actively expressed on earth, his ekklesia, his people living unashamedly as representatives of Christ, demonstrating, and proclaiming his whole gospel in every sector of life.

The dark circles represent the kingdom of darkness and the works of evil, the sin pandemic that has corrupted God's good creation—thoughts and actions that are not in alignment with God's goodness, and on a corporate level, corruption in business, racism in society, oppression in government and the like.

Now that we are no longer fragmenting the gospel, now that we are not shrinking God into either a religious or a social box, at last the whole gospel of the kingdom is being declared and demonstrated. Because of this the kingdom of darkness is being driven back, illustrated by the dark circle becoming less dark. It is still there. It will always be there until Christ returns. But the gates of Hades are not prevailing, not able to withstand the victorious advance of Christ's royal stewards! Instead, they are living out their secret calling, redeeming both people and culture.

But there's more! People who were lost in darkness now see the radiance of our light, and a magnet effect is unleashed! They are drawn out of darkness, drawn to the light and as they come, they are transformed.

Here lies the key to exponential revival, reformation and transformation of lives communities and nations:

Not only does the light of the whole, unshrunk, unmitigated and unleashed gospel illuminate whatever is dark around it but it is so beautiful, so lovely and freeing and healing and life-giving, that it also it becomes irresistible! When those outside see this supernatural, power-filled, love-driven beauty of complete good news, they will be *attracted*. They will be drawn to us as they were to Jesus (Matt. 4:25; Mark 2:15). This was Jesus' vision when he declared, "And I, when I am lifted up from the earth, will draw all people to myself" (John 12:32). This is the grand vision that was first declared over the nation of Israel and then of Christ's church, the New Jerusalem in the resurrection: "Nations will come to your light, and kings to the brightness of your dawn" (Isa. 60:3) and "The nations will walk by its light, and the kings of the earth will bring their splendor into it" (Rev. 21:24). While the complete fulfillment of this vision

> Christ's grand and glorious invitation is for us to live each day with the expectation of being not only lights in the darkness but magnets drawing others into life, healing and purpose.

will only be realized upon Christ's return, remember, his kingdom is here, now!

People will be attracted to what we are because we radiate his love, life and liberty. They will be transformed, healed, saved, and discipled. Addicts will be delivered, traffickers transformed into rescuers, poverty turned into bounty, orphans given loving homes. Churches and other kingdom communities will experience explosive growth and be celebrated as hubs of healing, "essential services" without which the community would again grow dark.

When we live as demonstrational witnesses, engaging in pre-discipleship, attraction and multiplication will happen. This is the power of your secret calling, unleashing the multiplied life and power of God's whole-life gospel, filling the earth with his goodness.

Full Circle—Cultivating and Keeping Guard

After commanding his disciples to "make disciples of all nations," Jesus added, "teaching them to observe all things that I have commanded" (Matt. 28:20 NKJV). We think Jesus is just telling us to obey, as a parent would warn a child not to lie or steal. Our English rendering of *tay-reh'-o* as merely "observe," "follow," or "obey" diminishes its magnificent meaning. *Tayreho*[1] is a synonym for *shaw-mehr*, or "keep guard," in Genesis 2! Thus, the Great Commission declares the Edenic commission restored. As a citizen of the kingdom, as a disciple, you are now authorized and deputized . . . to be a guardian of all that is good, an advocate for God's precious human beings, a steward of his purposes in the earth. But now there is an added glory! As the resurrected body is superhuman, so the restored kingdom on earth, the restored stewardship, is more glorious than the first! It is now imbued with the miraculous power of Christ's resurrection. The latter glory is greater than the former (Hag. 2:9).

When we dare to see the Great Commission this way, discipleship becomes the prerequisite of salvation and also the indispensable outworking of it, multiplying the momentum of the repeating *life* cycle of "on earth as it is in heaven."

Somebody is going to disciple the nations. If we don't, the devil will . . . and has been doing so for millennia.

> Fission—the divided kingdom in which we divorce God's spiritual goodness from his goodness in creation—is replaced by *fusion* power, the synapsis of the two into something miraculous, something **infinitely good** that results in both the healing of things in the temporal world and myriads more redeemed into the kingdom of light.

"Ask me, and I will make the nations your inheritance and the ends of the earth your possession" (Ps. 2:8). But we have not been asking for nations, only for a few souls extracted out of the nations. And then we lament that the devil is destroying both nations and souls. In one sector of the world we celebrate that revival is happening, only to see another sector slip into abject darkness, so that today there are more lost people than ever before. This is because we've been sharing and living a partial gospel.

We've been diverting eternal souls from hell into heaven but not discipling living people to bring heaven into earthly hells. And therefore fewer souls perceive heaven.

On the other hand, when we disciple people to bring heaven into earthly hells, then not just a few individuals but entire cities, seeing heaven in us, will en masse exodus the kingdom of hell and enter the kingdom of heaven.

Now that you are liberated to see the power of the full gospel, you can also believe and step into an undiminished, King-sized Great Commission! Each of the case studies has provided an example of what it looks like when we actuate the big, full gospel, the gospel of the kingdom, the greater Great Commission—our secret calling.

Let's conclude by looking at a few more practical steps that you can take to start living out your secret calling, to launch you into your adventure of unleashing God's highest purpose!

15

ENTER YOUR SECRET CALLING

"Ask me, and I will make the nations your inheritance and the ends of the earth your possession."
—Ps. 2:8

"Nations will come to your light, and kings to the brightness of your dawn."
—Isa. 60:3

"No more let sins and sorrows grow nor thorns infest the ground. He comes to make his blessings flow far as the curse is found."
—Isaac Watts

Rest in His Yoke

All this may seem overwhelming. You may be thinking, *Oh my gosh, where do I start?* Start by resting. Remember, Jesus said, "Take my yoke upon you and learn from me, for I am gentle and humble in heart, and you will find rest for your souls. For my yoke is easy and my burden is light" (Matt. 11:29–30).

Spend some time meditating on what you've read in these pages. Don't think about application yet. Soak in his presence as you allow this bigger understanding to come into focus. We're all on a journey. I myself am constantly seeing deeper insights into this mystery of God's incredible kingdom. So just let the Holy Spirit speak to you. Let him show it to you in his own way, in a way that is uniquely for you.

"Abide in me . . . I am the vine" (John 15:5). The branch doesn't struggle to stay attached to the vine. It just abides and through that relationship receives the flow of sap that brings forth leaves and fruit. Remember, relationship with him is the core. All else will come forth because you are an heir in the royal family.

> Your secret calling will flow not from striving but from resting in your Father-King's goodness, receiving his fullness, and letting it overflow.

WIN's native leaders are the incredible, courageous heroes who bring healing to broken lives and communities in remote, neglected regions. But an equally important part of WIN's work are our partners around the world who sacrificially provide prayer and funding. I often travel with our native leaders to check on projects and document outcomes so that our partners can see the fruit of their investments.

Reaching our project sites often requires hiking up steep slopes or driving motorbikes or jeeps over a thin strip of steep, rutted terrain not worthy of being called a road, that was recently cut into the edge of a mountain. The wheels churn and slide in the rocks and loose dirt barely a couple of feet from a sheer cliff into the abyss. Upon reaching a hairpin turn, the driver must bring the vehicle to a stop, back up, and jockey it around to keep from putting a wheel over the edge. And often, he is talking on his cell phone while doing so! As the near-gone brake pads screech on the drums, in such moments I can't help but check my readiness to meet Jesus in person!

In other areas, there is persecution and suffering. Our native leaders face the same opposition against the advance of the kingdom of life that was endured by the earliest followers of Christ—beatings, jailings, and sometimes martyrdom.

It would be easy to be fearful or discouraged in such circumstances. But when we walk restfully in Jesus' yoke, he sustains us, encourages us, and shows us the next step, and then the next, until we break out into the victory beyond. So rest. Don't fret. Let him lead you. This is his work, not yours . . . his highest purpose, not yours. And he will fulfill it through you.

Disciple the Gates

With his blood Jesus' victory canceled the curse. Legally, the way is now open for a grand exodus from the kingdom of death into the kingdom of life. But how will people see and turn "from darkness to light, and from the power of Satan to God?" (Acts 26:18) When we live out our secret calling. When we are radically relevant and transformational in the *here* through the power of our citizenship in the kingdom that is "not from here" (John 18:36 NKJV).

For those already citizens of the kingdom, the church facilities will now receive a greater purpose; they will be training grounds to "equip his people for works of service" (Eph 4:12) and hubs of engagement solving human problems, while unashamedly teaching the Word of God and soul salvation through faith in Jesus. In this way the organized church and the church facilities fulfill their secret calling, discipling the gates of society.

But for those who aren't ready to come to a program, remember, Jesus King of *all* held legislative ekklesia assembly—"church"—in all sorts of venues—bazaars, streets, hillsides, weddings, homes, and public buildings. What he founded is supra-religious. It is kingly, it is royal. He builds ekklesia, not synagogue. Jesus had "church" in the home of the chief sinner of the city. He had "church" in the street by ministering healing to the broken. He had "church" on a hillside by teaching the life-giving principles of God's kingdom. He had "church" in a Jewish synagogue. Paul had "church" in a pagan agora. Peter had "church" in the home of a Roman general.

Like the assemblies in the Bible, Christ's ekklesia is to assemble in the city gates, at the places of influence. Ekklesia can happen inside businesses, government structures, restaurants, bars, and nightclubs. Ekklesia can occur in a hay field, at sporting events, in public schools. Jesus went to all those places where the people are—which we have been indoctrinated to consider "worldly."

Notice that these gatherings weren't religiously structured. When Jesus or the apostles engaged with people and places where participants were not yet kingdom citizens, they didn't "lead a service." Had Jesus said, "Zacchaeus, I want to come to your house and hold a church service," the chief tax collector perched up in a tree probably would not have budged! And if Jesus had said, "Zacchaeus, you need to repent of your corruption and get saved," Zacchaeus would have run away! But Jesus proposed something practical and relational, not religious. Jesus turned dinner with a corrupt thief into an ekklesia experience where kingdom principles were taught, repentance happened naturally, and a soul was saved into God's kingdom of life.

Where can you assemble ekklesia? In what intriguing, unorthodox, and incredibly influential venues, physical or virtual, can you connect with one or more people around something that glorifies Christ and his righteousness? What opportunities open up when ekklesia doesn't have to be composed of three songs, a prayer, a sermon, and an offering? What would "being his witness" mean if you can do it through your profession, your university, your hobby, or online, in the midst of the people with whom you already rub shoulders?

Church leaders, how can your church community assemble in the gates, in the midst of the larger community? How can your existing church gathering transition to experience the vision of Jesus more fully when he defined his community with that powerful, influential, entire-life-impacting term *ekklesia*?

Influence Influencers

Given our bigger commission as kingdom representatives, not just redeemed sinners, believers and churches can now also raise our sights. We are not worms but royalty—sons and daughters, elected ambassadors of the King! So, while every church's ministry to the homeless is good and praiseworthy, let us not be content to only influence at the bottom of the mountain (Isa. 2:2). Jesus and Paul both engaged kings, and among their followers were influential community leaders and wealthy businesswomen (Luke 8:1–3; Acts 16:14; Rom. 16:2). Among Jesus' twelve disciples were business owners, government officers, and political activists at the time when he called them. The greatest Old Testament leaders were kings, queens, judges, billionaires, and prophets who advised kings.

Let us demolish the demonic pagan-gnostic defensive attitude that Christians should not endeavor to occupy places of earthly influence. It is good when the Lord raises believers to be in powerful positions. Those who pursue such appointments must remember, amid the tumult and temptations that will swirl around them, to "seek first his kingdom and his righteousness"(Matt. 6:33), to govern or create in alignment with the good King. They must "guard" from evil first their own hearts, and secondly the "garden," that piece of earth or sphere of influence over which they are allotted stewardship. Churches should not ignore but must rally around these individuals. We should encourage, celebrate, facilitate, and especially pray intently for them.

The church is to be a prophetic voice guiding society into alignment with the good King's will. In regard to civic matters, churches and pastors are not the head itself, but the neck that turns the head, wielders of the keys of the kingdom that rules all kingdoms. Meanwhile, others are called to be Abrahams, Isaacs, Jacobs, and Deborahs, patriarchs and matriarchs, exemplifying God's kingdom in the midst of human kingdoms, stewarding wealth and serving in roles of influence. Others are called to be Josephs, Daniels, Esthers, and Nehemiahs, administrating businesses, cities, and nations.

Notice in several of the case studies discussed earlier in this book, the church reached out to the city mayor or other civil servants. The Christ followers asked, "How can we serve? What is a need we can help meet?" That opened the hearts to trust and doors to opportunity, culminating in a beautiful teamwork. A whole-life healing occurred. Souls were saved, and pandemics were quelled.

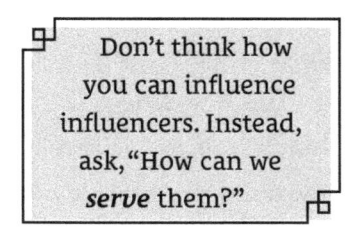

> Don't think how you can influence influencers. Instead, ask, "How can we *serve* them?"

Team Up

Jesus didn't say, "By this everyone will know that you are my disciples, if you have just the right doctrine." He said, "By this everyone will know that you are my disciples, if you love one another" (John 13:35). Some will contend, "But they speak in tongues!" "But they permit women to be pastors!" "But they are too seeker-sensitive!" "But they use liturgy." "But their worship is too emotional." "But they sprinkle instead of dunk." "But they pay respect to the Virgin Mary." *Stop!* Have grace! Grant honor! They are your brothers and sisters. You're going to spend eternity together, so might as well get over it now!

> The world is watching you. Do they see love or legalism? Don't be a Pharisee. If in doubt about where to draw the line, grant love preeminence over legalism.

Saint Augustine gave us a good rule of thumb: "In essentials, unity. In nonessentials, liberty. In all things, charity." Some who profess Christ have abandoned the core gospel message. If there is not unity in the essentials, then collaboration may still be possible, but only if it can happen without compromising an "essential."[1] Most everything else though, is a "nonessential." The enemy has handily kept us divided over the 1% in which we differ instead of united around the 99% in which we agree.

The few renegade reformers who endeavor to mobilize multiple churches to proclaim Christ, or to combat poverty or suicide in their city, often garner little interest. Why do churches have such a hard time collaborating? Because until now we've been operating on a partial gospel. In many cases doctrine isn't the main hindrance. We just don't see the urgency to work together on solving issues that are bigger than one of us can solve alone.

The time has come for us to align as do good kings when they resolve to stop the rampage of a terrorist regime. Maintaining autonomy, they meld their strength to bring about urgent deliverance.

One reason for the success of WIN's work is our discovery of the power of empowering others both inside and outside the body of Christ. In this way we are not building an empire but allowing Christ to build his kingdom. We are not influencing by mere addition but by multiplying leaders, resources, and vision across generations.

Your secret calling includes cultivating friendship and teamwork with those *not* inside your comfortable *oikos* (household or circle of friends) but who nevertheless embrace certain values of God's kingdom. A large corporation cannot be run by a handful of people. Neither can vast regions be reached, nor cities transformed, apart from collaboration. When kingdom communities grasp the bigger vision, they will no longer be factions arguing over doctrines. Neither will they be satisfied merely to join a network and attend a conference or two a year, but will seek out like-minded communities and actively collaborate on real initiatives. As we fulfill a mutual assignment such as combatting trafficking or poverty, friendship happens and we become peacemakers. As John Wesley said, "though we cannot think alike, may we not love alike? May we not be of one heart, though we are not of one opinion? Without all doubt, we may. Herein all the children of God may unite, notwithstanding these smaller differences."[2] If we are to fulfill God's highest purpose, we must team up.

> We think Jesus came to build churches and denominations on a foundation of doctrine, when in fact he came to build his ekklesia and his kingdom on the foundation of Christ.

The Urgency

Today the gates of Hades see some sectors of the church arising, and they are terrified because we hold the keys. So they are warring like never before, striving to prevail. Like the literal cavern at Caesarea Philippi alleged to be the gateway to the underworld, "Death expands its jaws, opening wide its mouth" (Isa. 5:14). The spiritual governors of the sin pandemic, all that is in opposition to the good Father King, are riding out upon the backs of deceived humans. They have at their command the masses as well as massive corporations who "[do] not know the Lord" (Judg. 2:10 NASB). Unwitting hosts of the sin-death pandemic, they are metamorphosed into enemies of the very goodness they believe they promote.

But freedom that is free of truth is lawlessness. It spawns everything that freedom isn't—racism, murder, oppression, and absolute slavery. The spiritual archons of death and their unwitting and bewitched hosts inspire corruption in human government, confusion of identity, and perversion of morality. They provoke legislation that promotes death while having the outward appearance of protecting lives, and wage war against the very heart of God. Entire sectors of the ekklesia are deceived into emasculating themselves by offering salvation without the cross, redemption without repentance, inheritance without responsibility.

But the darker the night, the brighter shines the light! Seeing that the "night is coming, when no one can work," Jesus didn't retreat; instead, he declared with a sense of urgency and passion, "As long as it is day, we must do the works of him who sent me" (John 9:4).

Of utmost importance remember this: "Our struggle is not against flesh and blood" (Eph. 6:12). Most humans who appear to collude with darkness are only pawns, hoodwinked and unwitting slaves of the sinister spiritual generals of the devil's sin-death pandemic. God's beloved human beings, and all of society, are not malefactors but victims. Jesus did not come to judge or condemn, but to save (John 3:17). Likewise, we are sent in his love and power to rescue, to protect, to guide—to heal!

A movement is afoot. Everywhere I turn, I see a holy fire kindling, and hear rustling in the trees as the wind of the Spirit approaches. As a new generation of the good King's ambassadors begin to live out their secret calling, Sauls will become Pauls, those most opposed to the kingdom will become its advocates, financiers and networkers.

Go!

The enemy wants to keep you from realizing how powerful you are. One-third of the world confesses Christ as Lord. What would happen if even a fraction of the world's 2.4 billion people grasped their secret calling and stepped forward to bring salvation, redemption, and hope, taking their place as royal healers? What if we turned our vision not primarily inward and upward but allowed our foundation in Christ to launch us outward—to the world around us? What if demonstrating Christ's love like he did—mingling with the people, participating in the culture not to concede to sin but to shine as a light—became a defining goal and a distinct purpose for every Christ follower and every congregation? What if believers today, like the early church, became known by our love for one another, by our disruptively higher way of life, being christened "the ones who hold the world together"?[3]

What if intentionally discipling our families, friends, workplaces, businesses, and governments resulted in people being attracted to us, drawn by the Presence that we radiate? What if our love, kindness, purity, servant leadership, excellence, as emancipators, innovators, and solutionists, became that for which we are known? What if this became that about which we talk and pray and develop strategies and initiatives? What if we did this in unity, as one body? Catholics and Presbyterians, Baptists, and Charismatics, not divided over what we disagree on but united around what we all hold sacred, that Jesus is Lord, and a wounded world needs his healing!

> What if the uniting of inner transformation with outward reformation resulted in a glorious demonstration of that for which the whole world longs—shalom, a whole-person, whole-life thriving?

What if our faith, lived boldly in the practical and the physical world, and also proclaimed unashamedly, opened wide those hearts which were once closed, which once said, "I'm not into religion" or "Christianity is irrelevant to life" but who now say, "I want what they have?"

What if that alignment with the heart of Jesus released a long-waiting deluge of favor upon each society practicing it until peace, honor, provision, and wholeness flowed?

By how great a span have we missed the mark for how many centuries! Yet how great an adventure now lies before us as we, embracing this revelation, step into the fullness of our inheritance! With Paul, we all confess, "Not that I have already obtained all this, or have already arrived at my goal, but I press on to take hold of that for which Christ Jesus took hold of me" (Phil. 3:12). This book is only an introduction to what could be a vast wonderland of discovering God's highest purpose: a multiplied experience of life here, life eternal, and ourselves as his royal healers sent into the world.

You are now ready to embark upon an adventure! Use the tools given in these pages, and let the Lord lead you into your calling, experiencing and fulfilling his highest purpose . . . which is no longer secret! Please do not go your way and forget what you've read. The situation is urgent. The trafficker has abducted God's beloved people. They are destined for destruction. But you are the King's hero. Find your sphere or spheres of influence. Receive his next steps and then take action. Walk with the King into your healing, stewarding, guarding destiny "as long as it is [still] day" (John 9:4).

Individuals, go forth into your secret calling as royal stewards, ambassadors elected to a royal post and sent to bring his kingdom of life wherever the kingdom of death is active. Leaders of churches, businesses and other kingdom communities, mobilize your team or congregation into God's highest purpose as his ekklesia, stewarding his kingdom on earth, discipling your city or jurisdiction of influence toward his goodness. Your team or church will no longer be sidelined or irrelevant.

You may be persecuted, but you'll also become an "essential service" and the lost whom you wondered how to reach, will be drawn to the brilliance of Christ that you radiate.

As kingdom citizens and all who love his goodness rise to this awesome future, a myriad will be saved, oppressors will become liberators, homeless will become home owners, victims will become victors, and nations will experience healing. When there is sufficient momentum, then this long-latent fusion, the long-awaited expression of God's kingdom in the earth will release the greatest Great Awakening in history. The way will be paved for the glorious return of King Jesus, for at last his highest purpose will be fulfilled, the proclamation by word and deed of "this gospel of the kingdom . . . in the whole world as a testimony to all nations" (Matt. 24:14).

ENDNOTES

Introduction
1. Robert Lynn, "Far as the Curse Is Found," *Breakpoint Worldview Magazine*, (October 2006): 14.
2. WIN (We Ignite Nations) is the organization of which the author is founder and president. Visit us at www.WIN.global and follow us @ weignitenations.

Chapter 1: The Secret Goodness
1. Visit us at www.WIN.global or @WeIgniteNations.
2. Vishal Mangalwadi, *The Book that Made Your World: How the Bible Created the Soul of Western Civilization*, (Nashville TN: Thomas Nelson, 2012). xxi.
3. Further reading: *The Case for a Creator* by Lee Strobel, *Return of the God Hypothesis* and *Darwin's Doubt* by Stephen C. Meyer, Institute for Creation Research, www.icr.org, Creation Ministries International www.creation.com and Answers in Genesis, www.answersingenesis.org.
4. *Evolution News*, "The Racism of Darwin and Darwinism," www.evolutionnews.org/2022/02/the-racism-of-darwin-and-darwinism, Accessed February 2024.
5. Alfred North Whitehead in a presentation at the Harvard University Lowell Lectures entitled "Science and the Modern World."
6. History.com, Galileo Galilei, www.history.com/topics/inventions/galileo-galilei, Accessed February 2024.
7. Strong's H2896. Blue letter Bible. https://www.blueletterbible.org/lexicon/h2896/niv/wlc/0-1/. For further reading see Scot McKnight and Laura Barringer, *A Church Called Tov: Forming a Goodness Culture That*

Resists Abuses of Power and Promotes Healing. (Nashville, TN: Tyndale House Publishers, 2020).
8   Dallas Willard and Gary Black, Jr. *Renewing the Christian Mind: Essays, Interviews, and Talks*, (New York, NY: HarperOne (Harper Collins), 2016), 17, https://www.amazon.com/Renewing-Christian-Mind-Essays-Interviews/dp/0062296132.
9   Strong's H7965.
10 Strong's H1515.
11 Tuvia Pollack, "Shalom in the Bible," The Bible Society in Israel, accessed January 26, 2024,
12 "Peace-Shalom (Hebrew Word Study)," Precept Austin, updated December 17, 2022, www.preceptaustin.org/shalom_-_definition.
13 Nicholas Wolterstorff, *Until Justice & Peace Embrace*, (Grand Rapids, MI: Eerdmans Publishing Co, 1983), 69 – 72.
14 Kevin Timmer, "Putting the 'And' Back into Gen. 2:15," in 2009 Proceedings of the Christian Engineering Education Conference.

Chapter 2: Your Triune Royalty
1   Westminster Shorter Catechism, Presbyterian Church in America, 355, accessed 2023, https://www.pcaac.org/wp-content/uploads/2019/11/ShorterCatechismwithScriptureProofs.pdf.
2   For this incredible testimony, read my first book, *Treasures in Dark Places: One Woman, a Supernatural God and a Mission to the Toughest Part of India* (Bloomington, Minnesota: Chosen Books (Baker Books), 2017).

Chapter 3: A Wounded World
1   Billy Graham, *Peace with God,* (Waco, TX: Word, 1953), 51.
2   www.WIN.global, @WeIgniteNations.

Chapter 4: Unshrinking Jesus
1   See Matt. 3:16–17, Isa. 61:1, and Luke 4:18.
2   Ibid.

Chapter 5: De-Fragmenting the Gospel
1   The Priene Inscription, Internet Archive, accessed 2023, https://web.archive.org/web/20170722070724/http://www.masseiana.org/priene.htm

2   See Integral Mission section in Lausanne Movement www.lausanne.org/tag/integral-mission; Wonsuk Ma and Brian Woolnough (Editors), *Holistic Mission: God's Plan for God's People* (Philadelphia PA: Fortress Press, 2010), Trevin Wax, Don't Let Holistic Mission Eclipse Evangelism, October 26, 2023, www.thegospelcoalition.org/blogs/trevin-wax/holistic-mission-evangelism, Accessed March 4, 2024

3   C. René Padilla quoted by David C. Kirkpatrick in Died: C. René Padilla, Father of Integral Mission, *Christianity Today* (April 27, 2021), Accessed 2023, https://www.christianitytoday.com/news/2021/april/rene-padilla-died-integral-mission-latin-american-theology.html.

Chapter 6: Case Study – Suicide to Shalom

1   Suicide, National Institute of Mental Health, accessed 2023, https://www.nimh.nih.gov/health/statistics/suicide. Joe Vaccarelli The Daily Sentinel Grand Junction Colorado (July 22, 2019), accessed 2023, https://www.gjsentinel.com/news/western_colorado/55-suicides-in-county-in-2018-coroner-calls-the-rate-disheartening/article_46cfd7e8-ac37-11e9-b334-20677ce05640.html.

Chapter 7: The Mystery Church

1   David Kinnaman and Gabe Lyons, *unChristian: What a New Generation Really Thinks about Christianity… and Why It Matters*, (Grand Rapids MI , Baker books: 2012): 223, https://www.amazon.com/unChristian-Generation-Really-Christianity-Matters/dp/0801072719

2   Less than half of Britons expected to tick 'Christian' in UK census – The Guardian, *The Defender*, (March 21, 2021), Accessed 2023, https://thedefenderngr.com/less-than-half-of-britons-expected-to-tick-christian-in-uk-census-the-guardian-uk.

3   Dallas Willard, *The Great Omission: Reclaiming Jesus's Essential Teachings on Discipleship*, (New York NY: HarperOne (Harper Collins), 2014), https://www.amazon.com/Great-Omission-Reclaiming-Essential-Discipleship/dp/0062311751.

4   "Why Do Young People Stay Christian?" Barna Group, Accessed 2023, https://www.barna.com/why-do-young-people-stay-christian.

5   "Church Dropouts Have Risen to 64%—But What About Those Who Stay?" Barna Group, accessed 2023, https://www.barna.com/research/resilient-disciples.

ENDNOTES

6 Adolf Harnack quoted in David J. Bosch *Transforming Mission: Paradigm Shifts in Theology of Mission*, (Maryknoll, NY: Orbis Books, 1991).58 PDF download here: https://www.academia.edu/44046109/_david_j_bosch_transforming_mission_a_paradigm , Original source: *The Expansion of Christianity in the First Three Centuries,* Volume 1, (New York: GP Putnam's Sons, 1904), 336-346 https://www.google.com/books/edition/The_Expansion_of_Christianity_in_the_Fir/oc1CAAAAIAAJ.

7 Hoekendijk. Original source: *Kirche und Volk in der deutschen Missionswissenschaft* (Munich: Kaiser, 1967), 245).

8 Tertullian, *Apology* Chapter 39, New Advent, Accessed 2023, https://www.newadvent.org/fathers/0301.htm.

9 Adolf von Harnack quoted by G. C. den Hertog in *The Ethics of the Early Church: What Can We Learn?* Christian Study Library, accessed 2023, https://www.christianstudylibrary.org/article/ethics-early-church-what-can-we-learn

10 Adolf Harnack quoted in Bosch. 58.

11 Adolf Harnack quoted in Bosch. 58.

12 Tertullian. *Apology* Chapter 39**.** Also see Adolf Harnack, *Mission and Expansion of Christianity in the First Three Centuries,* Chapter 4, Accessed 2023, https://www.ccel.org/ccel/harnack/mission.iv.iv.html#fna_iv.iv-p5.1.

13 Mathetes, The Epistle of Mathetes to Diognetus. Chapters 5 and 6, New Advent, Accessed 2023, https://www.newadvent.org/fathers/0101.htm.

14 Virginia Smith, *Clean: A History of Personal Hygiene and Purity*, (Oxford: Oxford University Press, 2008), 142, and Vivian Nutton, *Ancient Medicine*. (Oxfordshire: Routledge Press, 2012), 306–307.

15 For further reading, see: *How Christianity Changed the World* by Alvin Schmidt, *What If Jesus Had Never Been Born?* by Dr James Kennedy, *For the Glory of God* by Dr. Rodney Stark, and *Religion and the Rise of Western Culture* by Christopher Dawson.

16 Darrell L. Guder, *The Continuing Conversion of the Church*, (Grand Rapids: William B Eerdmans Publishing, 2000), 104.

17 David Bosch, Transforming Mission, 197.

18 Dallas Willard, *The Divine Conspiracy: Rediscovering our Hidden Life in God*, (New York NY: Harper Collins, 2014), Chapter 2.

19 K.L. Schmidt "E*kklesia," Theological Dictionary of the New Testament* Vol. III. Ed: Gerhard Kittel (Grand Rapids: William B Eerdmans Publishing. 1965), 516, https://www.google.com/books/edition/Theological_Dictionary_of_the_New_Testam/3YCXPigkZUkC In this quote, the word *cult* does not refer to a heretical sect that distorts foundational Christian doctrine, but to religious belief in general.
20 Blue letter Bible Lexicon: Strong's G1577 Ekklesia. https://www.blueletterbible.org/lexicon/g1577/kjv/tr/0-1/.
21 Patti Amsden, "Ekklesia: The Church – An Ekklesia Not a Syagogue," KingdomCongress.com, Accessed 2023, www.kingdomcongress.com/ekklesia-10-not-a-synagogue.html.

Chapter 8: Case Study – Welfare to Well-Being
1 To connect with Tony Kim, visit

Chapter 9: Your Secret Power
1 Dr Todd M Johnson, Christian Martyrdom: Who? Why? How?, Gordon Conwell Theological Seminary, https://www.gordonconwell.edu/blog/christian-martyrdom-who-why-how, Accessed March 2024.
2 Isaiah 9:6, Bible Hub, Accessed 2023, www.biblehub.com/commentaries/isaiah/9-6.htm.
3 Donald Drew, England Before and After Wesley. Disciple Nations Alliance, Accessed 2023, https://disciplenations.org/wp-content/uploads/2020/04/England-Before-and-After-Wesley_Drew.pdf. article from book by J. Wesley Bready, *England Before and After Wesley: The Evangelical Revival and Social Reform*. (Vancouver, BC: Regent College Publishing, 2021). See also David's Nine Inquiries Of The Lord (January 6, 2012), accessed 2024.
4 Jonathan Leeman, "The Relationship of Church and State," *The Gospel Coalition*, accessed 2023, www.thegospelcoalition.org/essay/the-relationship-of-church-and-state.
5 Check out Harvest Rock Church www.harvestrock.church, Harvest International Ministry www.harvestim.org, and Wagner University www.wagner.university.
6 Caitlin O'Kane, "We've been essential for 2,000 years:" California church holds service indoors despite coronavirus warnings, CBS News.

ENDNOTES

Updated on: July 20, 2020, accessed 2023, https://www.cbsnews.com/news/harvest-rock-church-california-coronavirus-lockdown-violation-services/.

7   Emily Hoeven, Why Churches Keep Winning Big against California, Cal Matters, (June 3, 2021), accessed 2023, www.calmatters.org/newsletters/whatmatters/2021/06/churches-win-lawsuits-against-california

8   Michael Gryboski, California to Pay $1.35M to Settle Harvest Rock Church Lawsuit against Gathering Restrictions, (May 20, 2021), accessed 2023, www.christianpost.com/news/calif-to-pay-135m-to-settle-churchs-lawsuit-over-covid-rules.html.

9   Harvest Rock Church, Inc. v. Newsom, CaseText.com, (May 14, 2021), https://casetext.com/case/harvest-rock-church-inc-v-newsom-4.

Chapter 10: Case Study – Evil Versus the Ekklesia

1   Arrest of Cali Mafia Leader Jose Santacruz-Londono, Legistorm.com, (July 5, 1995), accessed 2023, https://www.legistorm.com/stormfeed/view_rss/385570/organization/95775/title/arrest-of-cali-mafia-leader-jose-santacruz-londono.html.

2   Connect with Gisella, Marcy and Cali's Christian Community of Faith Church at www.comunifecali.org.

Chapter 11: Mind Shifts and the Three-P Key

1   Also see Patricia King, *Live Unoffendable: Free Your Heart to Find Healing, Empowerment and Joy*. (Maricopa, AZ: XP Publishing. 2022).

2   Joyce Meyer, *Blessed in the Mess: How to Experience God's Goodness in the Midst of Life's Pain*, (New York NY: Faith Words, 2023),48.

3   See www.WIN.global and follow our social media @WeIgniteNations.

4   Ed Silvoso, *Anointed for Business: How to Use Your Influence in the Marketplace to Change the World* (Ventura, CA: Regal Books, 2009), xix.

5   See Praxis Labs https://www.praxislabs.org/redemptive-entrepreneurship and Tyndale University https://www.tyndale.ca/cre.

6   Check out Jon's organization, Natural High www.NaturalHigh.org.

7   Check out Cutsforth Products at www.Cutsforth.com.

8   David Pyles, A Double Portion of Thy Spirit, The Berean Christian Bible Study Resources, http://www.bcbsr.com/survey/eli.html.

9   Rob Cutsforth, Interview 2023.

Chapter 13: Unleashing the Ekklesia
1. Ralph Winter, The Future of Evangelicals in Mission, *Mission Frontiers,* (September 01, 2007) https://www.missionfrontiers.org/issue/article/the-future-of-evangelicals-in-mission.
2. Charity, *Collins English Dictionary* online, https://www.collinsdictionary.com/us/dictionary/english/charity.

Chapter 14: The Key to Exponential Good
1. Strong's G5083.

Chapter 15: Enter Your Secret Calling
1. The "essentials" are primarily contained in the Nicene Creed.
2. The Epistle of Mathetes to Diognetus.
3. The Epistle of Mathetes to Diognetus.

BIBLIOGRAPHY

Bosch, David J. *Transforming Mission: Paradigm Shifts in Theology of Mission.* Maryknoll, NY: Orbis Books, 1991.

Cinquanta, Leanna. *Treasures in Dark Places: One Woman, a Supernatural God and a Mission to the Toughest Part of India.* Minneapolis, MN: Chosen Books (Baker Books), 2017.

Kinnaman, David and Gabe Lyons, *unChristian: What a New Generation Really Thinks about Christianity… and Why It Matters.* Grand Rapids MI: Baker Books: 2012.Vishal. *The Book that Made Your World: How the Bible Created the Soul of Western Civilization.* Nashville, TN: Thomas Nelson, 2012.

Miller. Darrow. *Discipling Nations: The Power of Truth to Transform Cultures.* Seattle, WA: YWAM Publishing, 1998.

Silvoso, Ed. *Ekklesia: Rediscovering God's Instrument for Global Transformation.* Minneapolis, MN: Chosen Books (Baker Books), 2017.

Willard, Dallas. *The Great Omission: Reclaiming Jesus's Essential Teachings on Discipleship.* New York NY: HarperOne (Harper Collins), 2014.

Wolterstorff, Nicholas. *Until Justice & Peace Embrace.* Grand Rapids, MI: Eerdmans Publishing Co, 1983.

Wright, N.T. The Challenge of Jesus: Rediscovering Who Jesus Was & Is. Westmont, IL: InterVarsity Press, 2021.

For further recommended reading, please see the Resources web page at www.LeannaCinquanta.com

ABOUT THE AUTHOR

A graduate of Youth With A Mission, Fuller Seminary, and Regent University, Dr. Leanna Cinquanta is a published author and the founder of We Ignite Nations (WIN). When not directing teams who rescue kids from traffickers, innovating ways to end poverty in whole communities, or equipping more world-changers, Leanna enjoys her horses in western Colorado.

IGNITING HOPE, EMPOWERING LIFE

WIN — WE IGNITE NATIONS

Founded by Leanna Cinquanta, We Ignite Nations (WIN) provides training, infrastructure and innovative solutions turning poverty into plenty and combatting human trafficking.

WIN IS:

- Not just putting food in people's mouths but empowering them to provide for their own families.

- Not just rescuing victims of human trafficking but training whole communities, creating "slavery-free zones."

- Not just educating underprivileged kids, but innovating sustainable solutions that end systemic poverty.

- Not just addressing temporal needs but building upon Christ, resulting in multidimensional peace, prosperity and purpose.

CREATE A WIN-WIN FUTURE.
LEARN MORE & GIVE ONLINE

WWW.WIN.GLOBAL
@WEIGNITENATIONS

Win is a US 501(c) three nonprofit organization

Treasures
IN DARK PLACES

This firsthand, often-supernatural account begins with Leanna's childhood and incredible face-to-face epiphany of Jesus. It then follows the rigors, heartaches, and miracles of a life propelled by faith into one of the poorest and darkest places on earth. Leanna's fearless determination to shine Jesus' light into the shadows--whether helping the destitute in small villages or rescuing children before they become victims of human trafficking, will inspire you to believe his power can change even your most trying circumstances.

"ABSOLUTELY RIVETING!"

"A MUST READ FOR ANYONE WITH GOD'S HEART FOR THE MOST VULNERABLE."

"A MASTERFULLY PAINTED ACCOUNT OF SACRIFICE AND TRIUMPH."

"COMPELLING, HEART WRENCHING AND BEAUTIFULLY WRITTEN."

A HARPER COLLINS EDITOR DECLARED THIS TO BE THE BEST TESTIMONIAL SHE HAD READ SINCE CORRIE TEN BOOM'S THE HIDING PLACE.

ONE WOMAN, A SUPERNATURAL GOD, AND A MISSION TO THE TOUGHEST PART OF INDIA

BY
LEANNA CINQUANTA

LEARN MORE AT
LeannaCinquanta.com